BASIS AND BELIEF

BASIS AND BELIEF

James Henry Collins

WIPF & STOCK · Eugene, Oregon

Wipf and Stock Publishers
199 W 8th Ave, Suite 3
Eugene, OR 97401

Basis and Belief
By Collins, James Henry
Copyright©1964 Methodist Publishing - Epworth Press
ISBN 13: 978-1-4982-0502-3
Publication date 8/28/2014
Previously published by Epworth Press, 1964

Every effort has been made to trace the current copyright owner of this publication but without success. If you have any information or interest in the copyright, please contact the publishers.

CONTENTS

1. THE GREEK CHALLENGE TO AUTHORITY AND ITS CONSEQUENCES 1
2. THE RISE OF AUTHORITARIANISM AND THE DECAY OF LEARNING 16
3. THE REVIVAL OF THE GREEK SPIRIT OF FREE ENQUIRY 23
4. THE MODERN CONFLICT TAKING SHAPE—THE PLACE OF AUTHORITY IN THE DEVELOPMENT OF MODERN THOUGHT 30
5. MODERN THEOLOGY AND THE PROBLEM OF AUTHORITY 57
6. A CRITIQUE OF RELIGIOUS AUTHORITY . . . 91
7. THE LEGITIMACY AND LIMITATIONS OF THE METHOD OF AUTHORITY IN RELIGION 127

BIBLIOGRAPHY 157

INDEX 160

CHAPTER ONE

THE GREEK CHALLENGE TO AUTHORITY AND ITS CONSEQUENCES

A MOVEMENT of the spirit of man, which was to have incalculable consequences for the future of mankind, began in a Greek city of Asia Minor in the sixth and fifth centuries before Christ. There a few men began to speculate about the whole situation of man in his world. What is the real nature of the world in which we find ourselves, and what is our relationship to it? Does the variety of the phenomena we see about us conceal any underlying unity or unifying principle. Can any satisfactory account of the world be given in terms of nature itself and without calling upon the aid of traditional and mythological factors which afford no satisfaction to a mind bent upon rational explanation? What is the origin of the human race, and how is it related to the animals and to the other living creatures which are its indubitable partners in the world? And what of the gods? Can they be included in such a scheme?

The answers which were given by the first scientist-philosophers of Greek Asia do not matter for our present purpose. In fact, Greek thought was very soon toying with the notion that the world is a manifold of incredibly small elements, that differences of quality and all other differences can be explained as differences of quantity, and that such a world can be analysed and expressed in mathematical terms. So that the movement which began with Thales, Anaximander and Anaximines soon led to a remarkable anticipation of the findings of modern physics. But the scientific insights of the Greeks had a precarious existence in the absence of relevant scientific techniques. The modern atomist is not directly indebted to Greek atomism. Modern atomic theory is a by-product of the experimental method rather than a grand hypothesis designed to elucidate the phenomenal complex which confronts humanity. It was not so much the content of Greek thought about the world, but its method and spirit, which set the pattern for philosophy for generations to come and inaugurated scientific explanation.

In the world which surrounded the comparatively small group of thinkers who developed and received and transmitted Greek ideas very different modes of explanation prevailed. Accretions of folk-lore and religious tradition had produced a body of 'authoritative' myths which purported to offer a quasi-historical account of man's place in the world and of the creation of the world itself. It was always a dangerous enterprise to challenge this kind of tradition and it may be of interest to inquire why the challenge came, in the first place, from Greek thinkers and a Greek civilization, and not from Persia, her great rival in the ancient world, or from the ubiquitous Semites, whose wisdom was regarded highly by the Greeks themselves.

As far as the Persians are concerned the answer is not easy to discover. It is no longer possible to argue from racial characteristics, for it is becoming obvious in the rapidly changing conditions of the modern world that enormous variations in racial behaviour are brought about by variations of environment. The right man needs the right moment and the right opportunity if he is to justify his potentiality. The Persians had no dearth of wise men and their religious insights in particular had enduring effects upon subsequent moral and spiritual ideas. They were capable of producing a distinctive literature and they were pioneers in the appreciation of painting and music and in the creation and enjoyment of lovely gardens. If it be argued that in spite of this they were never quite civilized, neither were the Greeks. But the Greeks were content with pockets of civilization at a time when Persia was following a policy of diffusion, and to spread Persian culture and discipline more widely they had to apply a good deal of governmental power and to exercise close supervision over every aspect of provincial life. There had been little opportunity before the settlement of Darius for vigorous and independent intellectual development, and when Darius succeeded in his plans to strengthen the empire he attributed his success to his religious orthodoxy, so that disloyalty to Ormuzd was henceforth likely to be mistaken for disloyalty to the king himself. This sort of thing does not encourage speculation. It should perhaps be added that the dualistic and non-anthropomorphic character of Zoroastrianism made it a possible substitute for philosophy, while Greek religion was less capable of affording intellectual satisfaction and cried out for the regulative force of philosophy.

THE GREEK CHALLENGE 3

In the Semitic world there was a still closer connexion between secular and spiritual power. 'The Semitic despot ruled, often only with the help of mercenaries, but also because he possessed, besides the accepted qualifications (e.g. pure blood, physical and other ability), some token of superhuman power or of divine recognition.'[1] Since the ruler ruled with the help of a divine power, he was under divine obligation, and his person and power were entitled to the respect which is due to sacred objects. The person of a Semitic king exhibits both the majesty of the incarnate power of his god, and the peculiar sanctity of the high priest who understands the ways of the god and is able to act as a mediator and convey the benefits of his unique standing with the god to his subjects. 'The Egyptian Ramses II "gives health to whom he will"; he sacrificed to the god Sutekh for fair weather and was popularly supposed to possess influence with his god' (ibid.). Behind the authority of the king, if all went well, was the derived authority of the official priesthood. In different peoples the precise development and expression of this relationship varied a great deal, as we would expect. The priestly caste in Egypt did not arise until the establishment of the college of Amon-Re in the seventeenth dynasty (ibid., p. 323). Before that a much freer and more improvised relationship existed between the dynasty and the irregular priesthood.

In Babylon regional government in the city-states was in the hands of the patesis or prince-priests and, not unnaturally, the high priests gained in power and importance and exercised secular power in the manner of the medieval bishop. Meanwhile, the central authority was linked to the life of the temple, which became the embodiment of secular dignity and authority as well as the symbol of religious devotion.

The situation in Israel was rather different. The intellectual achievements of modern Jews seems to suggest an endowment not unlike that of the Greeks, but the course of Jewish history provided conditions for intellectual development which were quite unlike those enjoyed by the thinkers of Greece. The familiar Semitic motif of the divinely sanctioned king reappears, but the religious background of his authority is an uneasy compound of austere Yahwism and the earthy, licentious religious practices inherited from the Canaanites. This state of affairs persisted throughout

[1] *Cambridge Ancient History*, I.213.

the period of the monarchy,[2] but it was always faced with the likelihood of a disruptive challenge from within. The challenge came from those redoubtable successors of the court magician, the prophets of Israel, who conceived Yahweh as a moral being whose holiness was only equalled by his power, and who was the Lord of History and the giver of the moral law. Within the prophetic framework great new ideas were incubated until, at length, the prophets of the eighth century began to envisage a religion which transcended national boundaries and interests, and called men to a concept of religion which counted social justice a primary ingredient of true worship. But although they were fearless men and stated their convictions against authority in circumstances of great personal danger, their efforts to liberate the spirit and institutions of their people were foredoomed. Semitic conservatism disguised the new thought as old tradition and the authority of the written law took the place of the fiat of an inspired sovereign.

In the Hellenic world, at the beginning of the speculative period, a very different set of conditions existed. Dr Gilbert Murray has said of Greek civilization that, 'To an extraordinary degree it starts clean from nature, with almost no entanglement of elaborate creeds and customs and traditions'.[3] The people we call Greeks were, like modern Britons, a racial amalgam. They had developed their national identity in a land whose geography favoured local autonomy, so that even on the Greek mainland there grew up side by side wide varieties of religious and political tradition. But the Greek world was not confined to the life of the peninsula. The early, formative invasions from the north had precipitated a widespread migratory movement which established Greek settlements in many parts of Asia adjacent to the Aegean. Later, in the eighth and seventh centuries, the pressure of unsatisfactory economic and political conditions at home led to a further migration and to the founding of Greek colonies stretching from the Black Sea and the Adriatic to the coast of North Africa.

In this scattered community the desire for free development had been happily matched by the means and the resolution to attain it. We have seen in our own times how profoundly traditional ways of life are affected by migration and colonization. In

[2] See Oesterley and Robinson, *Hebrew Religion* (S.P.C.K., 1930), p. 192.
[3] *The Legacy of Greece* (Oxford, 1922), p. 16.

the United States there are some hundreds of recognized religious denominations and sects. The main streams of Catholic and Protestant Christianity persist in a more or less unmodified form, but around them an extraordinary collection of strange and sometimes highly improbable varieties have sprung up. We do not need to look far to find the roots of this prolific growth of free religious forms. It has developed in association with a mixing of races, a mixing of primary religious sources, a new environment, the strains and demands of a new and growing society, and the opportunity afforded by the severance of all but the most tenuous connexions between the Constitution and a particular religious point of view.

The politico-religious situation in many parts of the scattered Greek communities of the sixth and fifth centuries provided a similar opportunity. The mythological corpus was challengeable because it had no official custodians and interpreters whose conclusions could be enforced by the executioner. In his original state of patriarchy the virtue of a Greek was to obey, but subsequent pressures had set aside first the king and then the noble few as the sources of law and authority, and there had been established, in many cases, a merchant aristocracy which was more interested in the maintenance of prosperity than in the perpetuation of theories of government. Where the oligarchic stage had been succeeded by tyranny there was an even greater tendency to dispense with the traditional moral and religious supports of society and to encourage only those observances and customs which tended to stabilize the new order, or which would at least be innocuous to it. Where intellectual activity constituted no direct threat to the régime, and this was generally the case, the tyrants extended their patronage.

The democracy of classical Athens is said to mark the highest point of Greek emancipation (though not the best period of Greek government, according to Aristotle). 'They revelled in a freedom within the framework of mutually advantageous law which was the envy of their neighbours',[4] or so Thucydides made Pericles claim on their behalf. Here at last, it would appear, is the environment in which freedom and truth can be pursued without obstacle. Here seems to be the milieu where the restraining hand of the past has very little power, a society where aspiration may rise

[4] *History of the Peloponnesian War*, II.37.

unchecked and the pursuit of truth be unhindered by the fear that its discovery will bring harm to the established order. But unlimited democracy, as Socrates found, has its own bad reasons for inhibiting the freedom of philosophers; especially if it happens to be a democracy that still fingers the scars of recent oppression.

We have contrasted the situation of the Greeks with that of their rivals in the ancient world in order to indicate an important factor in their bid for true freedom of the mind. Where a rigid religious tradition is supported by the power of an absolute ruler speculation is inhibited, or tends to confine itself to the permitted areas. This will become more and more apparent as later authoritarian systems are examined. But men with courage and marked individuality who have once tasted the adventure of free mental discourse will not easily submit to an arbitrary restriction of intellectual activity simply because times have changed and society has become less sympathetic toward philosophical innovators. In the earliest stages of Greek thought there may have been no problems of freedom simply because there was little apparent social relevance. It is unlikely that the people of Miletos realized what was implied by the scientific excursions of their thinkers. Their work seems to have been disarmingly traditional in style and, in any case, the problem of ultimate reality must have seemed to their contemporaries to be comfortably remote from the business and security of the city. In fifth-century Athens, however, philosophy spoke the language of the market-place and the assembly and gradually turned its attention from physical speculation to the field of human relationships, human conduct, and human destiny. These were more perilous topics. It is true that Anaxagoras had been condemned and exiled for impious speculations about the solar system, but it appears that his real crime was not astronomical impiety but friendship with Pericles at an unfortunate juncture of that great man's career.

The scientists had duly challenged the traditional world picture and had substituted simplifications which were quite incredible to the generality of citizens, but not particularly upsetting. After all, it did not matter too much how a scientist chose to describe the world substance. All things might very well be a logical unity, as Parmenides had said, or, as Anaxagoras claimed, the world might be constructed from an immense number of qualitatively differentiated particles. If you were a mathematician like Pythagoras it was natural enough to see quantitative differences in steps and to construct a world of numbers. But hypotheses about numbers and air and fire and water and evolution did not impinge directly upon the life of the city. They were all consistent with the common-sense view of life, or if they were not, a Zeno would make nonsense of them. In the meantime, a jug of wine remained, to philosopher and layman alike, an indubitable jug of wine. Traditions of a more tender kind, however, were challenged by the Sophists. Many of the less notable of the Sophists may have been little more than private tutors in miscellaneous subjects, but Plato's impression of Protagoras[5] suggests that the best of them sought to inculcate the special abilities which would fit a young man to make a success of life in a democratic city-state. But there was a strong body of opinion hostile to the Sophists and fearful of the consequences of their activity. Like Socrates, who was bracketed with them by other people besides Anytus, they were suspected of bringing ruin and corruption to all who associated with them.[6]

This hostility was reflected in the charge against Socrates, who was indicted in terms which identify him, in the minds of his accusers, with the Sophist movement. The specific charge against him was that he had corrupted young men and defied religious tradition,[7] whilst the general terms of the popular charge against him, as he himself is made to formulate it, alleged that he indulged an impious curiosity and that he perverted truth by his skill in argument. (ibid., 19b). Apart from the misplaced charge about scientific experiments, these are all matters which identify Socrates, in the popular mind, with the Sophist movement, and it is to be noticed that in his defence he was at pains to dissociate himself from the Sophists. He preferred to regard himself as an amateur and a seeker of wisdom, not as a professional teacher of wisdom.

The Sophists seem to have initiated the kind of work which Socrates and Plato developed so admirably. They hammered language into a keener tool and revealed the usefulness of logic to demolish pretensions. Burnet[8] challenged the older view that because Protagoras was a relativist his teaching contained a threat to established notions, not only about nature, but about morality

---

[5] *Protagoras*, 318c, ff. [6] *Meno*, 91c. [7] *Apology*, 24b.
[8] *Greek Philosophy, Thales to Plato*, pp. 114ff.

and society; 'So far from being a revolutionary, he was a champion of traditional morality, not from old-fashioned prejudice, but from a strong belief in the value of social conventions (ibid., p. 117). The danger of the Sophist movement from the point of view of established society was precisely that it sought to turn men away from speculation about nature, where new techniques of investigation were needed before any real progress could be made, and to focus philosophical endeavour on the conduct of human affairs. Socrates represents the summit of this tendency.

The conflict between Socrates and the city of Athens is of interest to this study precisely because the decision which was hammered out before his judges was intended to declare, from the point of view of the State, how necessary it was to defend public tradition and authority against the mischief of private doctrines which might cast doubt upon the public repository of wisdom. From many points of view the religious and political traditions of Athens were remarkably flexible, but the verdict of the dicastery was none the less a verdict upon private judgement whenever private judgement should come into conflict with the authority of law and tradition. The ordinary Athenian citizens who heard the charges against Socrates would not be likely to distinguish between an attack on dogmatic prejudice and an attack on the law and custom of the city itself. In his person they saw an embodiment of the spirit of restless interrogation of motive and purpose which had succeeded the ontological questionings of the scientists, together with an uncomfortably vivid religious consciousness which derided and threatened the neat, formal pattern of their own observances. Moreover, they saw these factors united in a man whose friends had included active enemies of the democracy. These things alone would have made his condemnation likely, but the deciding factor was the attitude of Socrates himself. The story, as Plato tells it, moves in the deep grooves of tragedy. There is insufficient contact between the views and aims of the contesting parties for the issues at stake to be truly evaluated. The accusers push on, through allegations of atheism and corruption and their own turbid fear of political reaction, to a sentence of death whose execution they can hardly have anticipated. Socrates, on the other hand, goes on his self-appointed way as untouched by fear of personal harm as he was among the hoplites of Potidea. He even neglects the obvious and prudent measures of defence which

THE GREEK CHALLENGE 9

lie close to his hand. The issue for him is one of his own making.[9] He will not accept life at the price of an arbitrary limitation of his freedom to search for truth by his own chosen method of dialectic; nor will he accept freedom anywhere else but in the city where freedom belongs.

In the Crito, however, we see that Socrates had a very real regard for the authority of the State as embodied in its laws. He had no doubt that the men who condemned him had acted unjustly, but neither did he doubt that the sentence they had passed on him had the force of law. And by that law, the law of Athens, which he had freely contracted to obey, he considered himself to be bound.[10] To subvert the law of the city was to jeopardize the security of the State, and Socrates loved Athens far too well to pursue such a course even though his own life hung upon the decision. Since this was his attitude, it is even more remarkable that he denied absolutely to the government, whether for the time being oligarchic or democratic in form, the right to dictate to him on matters of conscience, or to divert him from his mission to seek truth.

The stand which Socrates made probably represents the highwater mark of spiritual freedom in Greek thought. After his death the tide receded a little. According to Robin,[11] the method of Socrates liberated the conscience from the restraints of traditional authority. It seems, however, on the evidence of his own statements, that the emphasis of his work was on the destruction of false opinion and ill-founded pretensions to knowledge. The protagonist of a critical method like this may find it easy to dispense with authority and tradition, but when criticism has done its preliminary work of demolition the work of construction must begin, and here it is much more difficult to break free from the traditional forms and restraints. This becomes apparent when we move from Plato's account of his master to his own constructive teaching. The *Republic* was probably not an entirely serious attempt to provide a blue-print for society but an attempt to envisage the application of philosophical principles to the structure of society; the magnitude and range of the society being drawn to the scale with which Plato was most familiar. The result is uncompromisingly authoritarian. The authority is virtuous and benevolent, but for the very reason that it rules in

[9] *Apology*, 29c-30c.   [10] *Crito*, 52f.   [11] *Greek Thought*, p. 159.

the interest and by the power of goodness and wisdom, it cannot allow freedom: for freedom would necessarily be freedom in the direction of wickedness. In order to produce the right human material for the government and defence of the country, or the community, Plato is prepared to tie all artistic and intellectual activities to the supposed advantage of the State. Existing literature must be modified to exclude unedifying stories about the gods,[12] for stories about the gods must illustrate the theological assertion that God is the source of good only (ibid., 380). The legendary heroes must be trimmed to ideal proportions and if they have ever been caught in an undignified situation, or if the gods have ever been portrayed in a mood of unbecoming levity, the record must now be suppressed. Musical modes and rhythms are to be sifted to eliminate tendencies to softness and melancholy (ibid., 398ff), the visual arts must be allowed to represent only good character and conduct (ibid., 401), while new literary traditions, embodying the right values, may be invented and presented to the people in the guise of authoritative myths in order to secure loyalty to the State (ibid., 415).

Loss of liberty is everywhere in the *Republic*, but the absence of liberty was unremarkable in the ancient world. Plato demands that the person of the subject be at the disposal of the State, and in his system, unlike most modern autocratic variants, the individual who becomes distinguished by qualities and training, and is consequently a person of importance to the State, has even less freedom. The alarming feature of the scheme is its disregard for the very freedom of speculation which made Plato's own work possible. Men are not to be trusted to have reactions of their own to the great literature which has evidently not corrupted Plato, for he is claiming for himself, though the dramatic character of Socrates, a directive authority sanctioned by a special relationship to truth. If the philosopher-king possesses an unlimited store of wisdom and virtue, a good deal can surely be claimed for the philosopher who envisages him before he exists. But no doubt Plato would have insisted that such aristocratic sovereignty did exist already in the normative realm of ideas. In other words, Plato's authoritarianism is a consequence of his general metaphysical position. Ordinary people who are unable to see beyond the visible phenomena of the world about them are only able to

[12] *Republic*, 378f.

reach a tentative half-knowledge of things. Plato calls this 'belief' or 'opinion' (ibid., 479), whereas the philosopher, who sees the unchanging world of the forms, has true knowledge. It is apparent, therefore, that the philosopher-king, who unites the choice of the State with the pure wisdom which looks upon the face of reality itself, will possess unlimited authority. His authority rests upon the supremely real, the form of the good itself, and he himself acquires, as far as humanly possible, the characteristics of the divine order which he himself perceives and mediates (ibid., 500).

It is easy, however, to misconstrue what Plato has to say about freedom and authority. His suspicion of democratic freedom is rooted in the conviction that it is not true freedom. True freedom is to be found only in correspondence with final reality—τὸ ὄντως ὄντων—the philosopher's goal. All other seeming varieties of freedom are only differing forms of bondage, since they tie life and action to opinion at the best and error at the worst. A life which is informed and directed by the Good is, on Plato's premisses, entitled to unlimited authority, for its authority is the imperative inherent in things as they really are. To deny such authority is to misconceive the order of the universe. If such a source of light were accessible, we might indeed be willing to live in its brightness and to find there the perfection of freedom united with perfect conformity. But there have been few men who could have put forward a plausible claim to this kind of self-identification with reality, while the men who have sought to impose their authority upon the world have for the most part been manifestly out of touch with the form of the Good. Plato's authoritarianism, in fact, is the claim of the human spirit to be free from everything but the authority of the Good itself; for the only possible conclusion that can be drawn from his search for an ideal ruler, in the face of all that we know of human nature, is that no suitable candidate exists. In that case we are bound to obey no other will, but we must pursue the truth for ourselves.

Aristotle, too, was prepared to concede authority to the supremely good man, if he could be found. But he did not believe in the ideal existence of such a paragon and he was sceptical about his mundane existence. In consequence, in the Politics there is a good deal of unsatisfactory rummaging to find a reasonable second-best. Again, it is doubtful if Aristotle allows for true freedom of the mind. Education is not circumscribed so carefully as it is in the Republic, but care is to be taken to fit the individual to the State by judicious training.[13] Yet Aristotle is quite clear that the State exists for the sake of the good life (ibid., III.9.viii-xv), and the good life is individual before it is corporate. He strives, in true Greek fashion, to establish the authority of truth itself; to discover a principle of regulation which has a rational basis. Neither the actions of a tyrant nor the enactments of a democracy are to be considered just because they are edicts of superior power, on the one hand, or of constitutional authority on the other (ibid., III.10). Both must be measured by a standard of right and wrong which they did not create and cannot destroy, a standard which seems to transcend the actual order of the community in a way that resembles the Platonic forms. The metaphysical standpoint has changed a little, and reality has moved from the intelligible to the sensible world, but form is still the moulder of the world of experience, and potentiality is the comprehensive aspect of that which can be moulded, and this applies to societies as well as oak trees.

It is clear, then, that although Plato and Aristotle were prepared to countenance the use of authority in an effort to secure either an ideal state of society or, in the case of Aristotle, a working compromise, their metaphysical presuppositions made obedience to human authority difficult, especially in matters which concern the mind and spirit. They were prepared to use the device of authority to shape men and society. They were even prepared to restrict free access to learning where the content of traditional learning might prove subversive. But we must assume that they would have continued to recognize that freedom to criticize and to speculate in their own characteristic manner was a duty and a fundamental right for civilized men. The glory of Greek thought is not that Greek thinkers were usually right but that they demonstrated the need for thought to be unfettered and for curiosity to be unafraid of revealing deficiencies in the established order. The Greeks of the classical period challenged all authority everywhere and ever since by their assertion of the right of a man to stand on his own feet, to see facts with his own eyes, and to reach and announce his own conclusions.

There is no point in following the Greek story much farther.

[13] *Politics*, VIII.1.ii.

The teaching of the Socratics, and later of their lineal descendants the Stoics and Epicureans, reiterated man's right to construct his own intellectual picture of the world and his relationship to it, as well as seeking to enable him to adjust his life to the new political situation which followed the breakdown of the city-state, the loss of Greek independence, and the growth of Roman hegemony. At the same time a wider social environment tended to encourage a feeling of isolation in the individual, and philosophy was required to furnish a formula to reconcile men, singly and collectively, to the new situation. This was done by invoking different aspects of Socratic-Platonic teaching, and the answers which were obtained were surprisingly different. The two leading resultant forms, Stoicism and Epicureanism, had very different attitudes toward authority. Stoicism inherited the monism of Parmenides and translated it into a moral code and a mode of life. It first deified the world and then submitted to it, trusting to its purposefulness. Theoretically, the Stoic respected and obeyed the authority of developed society as a manifestation of the divine will, but in practice, his belief in the supremacy of the demands of conscience insulated the sage from the coerciveness of all local manifestations of authority. The Epicureans, for their part, sought escape from the pressure of unruly events in a cultivated attitude of detachment. Epicurus conceived the world in terms of a pluralism like that of Democritus, but devoid of the regulative force of law. His world, in consequence, was a chance assemblage, a miscellany in which a man may claim the sanctuary of inviolable privacy, without obligation or responsibility either to gods or men.

Beyond this point the philosophical impulse of Greece has flowed on, but in a wider stream. Inevitably, some of the original force and purity of its ideas have become diluted, but the assumption of the possibility and, indeed, the duty of rationality has persisted. Sometimes the dangerous Greek element has been petrified and permitted only a fossil existence in the core of authoritarian societies, but it has never been altogether forgotten, and has never lost the ability to break out again, with undiminished vigour, to challenge the irrationalism with which we seek, from time to time, to disguise our ignorance and to secure for ourselves privilege and authority to which we have no reasonable title.

It was possible for Greek thought to continue its course even when Rome became supreme. Roman power was secure and moderate in its heyday and it did not, in any case, feel that it was challenged in any way by the speculative tendencies of the Greeks. Moreover, the range of the earlier thinkers was only occasionally apparent in the philosophical predilections of the Greco-Roman period. It is sometimes assumed that Christianity put Greek thought quietly to death and that this fact is represented, at least symbolically, by Justinian's abolition of the Academy. But we know now that the Greek spirit was not killed then or at any later time, while the Neo-Platonism which was removed by this official interference was already moribund and unprogressive and owed more to Eastern mysticism than to the traditions of the Academy.

In the early years of the growth of the Christian Church Greek influence persisted and played a considerable part in the shaping of Christian doctrine. Many of the early Christian thinkers were men, like Clement of Alexandria, with a background of Greek culture; men who, as a matter of course, tended to re-think Christian dogma in terms of the philosophical doctrines which were familiar to them. We find, for instance, in the Christological controversies of the early centuries, that the two contending schools of thought, Antioch and Alexandria, illustrate the consequences of the application of two different categories of Greek thought to a problem of Christian doctrine. Antiochene Aristotelianism is represented by Paul of Samosata who, 'unlike the Alexandrians, finds his chief interest in the concrete and particular, not in the abstract and general, in the scientific analysis of human nature rather than in the metaphysical principles of which it is, or may be, the embodiment, in the study of the facts of history and experience more than the eternal relationships by which these facts are to be interpreted'.[14] Alexandrian orthodoxy, on the other hand, was rooted in the unmistakable Platonism of Origen. In this way the long debate of the Academics and Peripatetics was continued in the new media which Christianity provided. This was only the beginning of a process which helped to shape and guide the subsequent development of Christian theology. For a long time Platonism was dominant until the Aristotelian revival of the thirteenth century, and after that an uneasy mixture of Platonism and Aristotelianism became the official philosophy of Catholic

[14] C. E. Raven, *Apollinarianism* (Cambridge, 1923), p. 55.

Christianity. The debate did not end there. Christian Platonism flowered again in England in the seventeenth and eighteenth centuries, while in the nineteenth century biblical criticism brought a new and much more drastic application of Aristotelian method to bear on the source materials of Christian history.

CHAPTER TWO

THE RISE OF AUTHORITARIANISM AND THE DECAY OF LEARNING

WE MUST NOW consider why the lively intellectual discourse of early Christianity gave place to a long period of reaction and stagnation; why the champions of liberty soon became the officers of a new oppression; and why the new western society, which began to take shape, and in which the power of the church was so great, was tormented not only by the maladies of ignorance and superstition, but by the weapons of fear and cruelty.

While the Christian churches were still chiefly regional in their influence, and while they still suffered as a persecuted minority, the fathers were champions of toleration. But when the Church became established as the supreme intellectual and spiritual authority of the Empire and added temporal power to its authority, freedom was vigorously suppressed. The truth of these two propositions is not generally disputed,[1] and there is a temptation to leap to the conclusion that this sustained phase of intellectual attrition and suppression was quite simply the deliberate contrivance of a clerical power which was determined to exploit its advantages to the full. This must be a part of the truth. It is doubtful whether it is the most significant part. Much of the stiffening of theological formulae and the proscription of error was the result of a sincere regard for truth coupled with the conviction that truth was a depositum to be found only within the borders of orthodoxy. The earlier and more flexible stage of Christian theology came in a period of relative local autonomy, when local churches had, at most, a regional authority and were not subject to central government. But soon the organizational trend of the Church shifted the centre of power away from the local centres whose power was a reflection of the power of the city-states of the earlier empire, and followed the empire itself into hegemony, especially after the establishment of Roman ascendancy within the Church. New external relationships and the struggle for

[1] Cf. Lecky's *History of the Rise and Influence of Rationalism in Europe*, II.11ff.

THE RISE OF AUTHORITARIANISM

internal power made it increasingly difficult for theological disputes to be divorced from considerations of secular convenience and personal advantage. By the fifth century a degeneration is evident in the quality of the Church. The case of St John Chrysostom may serve to show the way political advantage began to outweigh theological integrity. In this conflict 'only a modicum of doctrinal enmity was mingled with personal rivalry and ambition'.[2] The same sort of pattern is perceptible in the events which led to the condemnation of Nestorius. It was becoming clear that to establish the truth of a theological point of view it was necessary to find friends at court.

To some extent this was due to the fact that the Christian religion was closely associated with Roman imperial power. We have observed the same tendencies to repressive authoritarianism in earlier societies where the alliance between the priest and the king was close, and from the time of Constantine the closest association prevailed, almost without a break, between the Christian Church and the empire, with far-reaching consequences both for the State and the Christian religion. From the imperial point of view this state of affairs 'intensified the hieratic cast of governmental authority',[3] but from the ecclesiastical point of view the result was much more serious. The linkage of power placed within reach of the all-too-human protagonists of the faith the whole armour of man, and began a process which was to make political and military power the yardstick of truth. From this beginning it was only a short step to the Caesaropapism of Justinian, who was determined not only to restore the order and glory of the Empire, but to tidy up the face of Christian theology at the same time. Justinian's activities illustrate the danger of combining religious zeal with political absolutism. It has always been tempting for men to assume that the possession of economic or political power entitles them to claim special attention and respect for their religious views. In Justinian's case the relative success of his efforts to restore the power of the empire encouraged him to seek to impose uniformity of belief and worship in the church which was an adjunct of his imperial power. The degree of success which came his way showed how easy it could be for an earnest theologian with a sufficiently large army to regulate theological opinion.

[2] *Cambridge Shorter Medieval History*, I.116.
[3] Moss, *The Birth of the Middle Ages* (Oxford, 1935), p. 250.

From the purely ecclesiastical point of view also, there was a marked preoccupation with power, for if emperors wanted to be popes, no less did popes wish to become emperors, or at least to wield a great deal of secular power, and when the spiritual and secular powers were in agreement the force of authority was oppressively great. As early as the end of the fifth century Pope Gelasius I was in a position to claim, in a letter to the emperor, that the world was under the dominion of two powers, 'the sacred authority of the pontiffs and the royal power'. Of the two, he judged the authority of the popes to be primary.[4] The claim of supremacy for the authority of the church does not seem to have been allowed until a much later date, but the Church grew and prospered under the shelter of the State: 'The church was a department of the state; the Emperor was head of the church, the Patriarch his Minister for Religion.'[5] Thus the Church had the opportunity to study absolutism at close quarters, while the Pope also had the opportunity to rehearse the application of power of the more immediate sort both as secular ruler of the Roman State and as the human vehicle through which the power of God was presumed to be given to kings and emperors. Even Charlemagne seems to have accepted the derived stature which this arrangement implies, though he managed to transform the significance of his coronation and established a theocracy which, in its turn, served as a model for the later Papacy.[6]

But if there was an external model for the Church's authority, the reasons which prompted the resort to authority were mostly of internal origin. So many heretical variations of Christian doctrine were traceable to the after-effects of Greek rationalism that the method of arriving at doctrinal definitions by consultation and disputation was felt to be impracticable. 'Men could not long rest amid the conflict of opposing arguments; they could not endure that measure of doubt which is the necessary accompaniment of controversy.'[7] Nor indeed could controversy be admissible when the notion of exclusive salvation was once established. If the church alone could offer the means of salvation, and if the functions of the Church rested upon the theoretical foundations of its dogma, then to dispute or even debate the dogmatic foundation

---

[4] *Cambridge Shorter Medieval History*, I.125.
[5] Moss, op. cit., p. 23.
[6] *Cambridge Shorter Medieval History*, I.318.   [7] Lecky, op. cit., I.381.

was to endanger the souls of men. 'As long as the doctrine of exclusive salvation was believed and realized, it was necessary for the peace of mankind that they should be absolutely certain of the truth of what they believed; in order to be so certain, it was necessary to suppress adverse arguments; and in order to effect this object, it was necessary that there should be no critical or sceptical spirit in Europe.' (ibid., p. 398). The price that was paid for this attitude was high. Once the truth has been appropriated and dedicated to a task which is held to be more important than itself, it is almost inevitable that the notion of truth will become utilitarian. When this happens, authority is at liberty to fabricate data quite freely in order to establish its position, and the resulting 'tradition' will itself be guaranteed as truth. The havoc which this kind of thing wrought in the minds of men during the whole period of the middle ages was enormous, for although we shall see that a few individuals conceived a love of truth for its own sake and were brave enough to seek it at great personal risk, most men were content or obliged to be docile under instruction and to receive truth upon authority. But perhaps this is still the case.

Unhappily, the régime of authoritarianism, with its unhappy concomitants of bigotry and persecution and its secondary products of pathogenic cruelty and sycophancy, was outwardly successful for a long time. The seeker of intellectual freedom within an authoritarian system is at a double disadvantage. Not only is the climate of opinion initially against his point of view, as is the case with any innovator, but the nature of his opponents' case forbids opposition. The disputant who proceeds from the assumption that he should not be contradicted and cannot be proved wrong without offence to the Almighty, is a difficult opponent to handle; and this was the strength of the theocratic society which took hold of the West while the new pattern of European life was emerging at the threshold of the middle ages. At its best times, and in its best parts, the theocratic State was a benevolent authority. There was a long period when active persecution waned, but that is only a measure of the relative success of the method of authority. Most of the subjects of the new empire would have agreed with Thrasymachus that justice is that which serves the advantage of the stronger party.[8] There is a point where tyranny becomes so well established that it no longer needs

[8] *Republic*, I.338c.

to be tyrannical, and this particular tyranny mellowed. Personal saintliness in some of its agents helped to conceal the fundamental error of its basis. Liberty is not less sweet when an Augustine condemns it, but in the aftermath, when the freshness of liberty is forgotten, captivity can be made more tolerable by his company. Perhaps this is why Lecky does not regard the medieval outcome as a tyrannical society, since it provided all the intellectual latitude that the generality of the people demanded (op. cit., II.28). It is true that the ideal of 'soldierly submissiveness' had become general, but we fail to see how a tyranny which eventually silences all opposition and becomes so difficult to challenge that it is obeyed without demur by nearly everyone, is any less a tyranny because it is successful. At that rate thieves would cease to be thieves whenever prosperity enabled them to abandon the active exercise of their profession and they were able to settle down and enjoy the profits.

On the other hand, it would be a mistake to ascribe the restrictive authoritarianism of the dark and the middle ages to the effects of Christianity on post-Roman society in Europe. As the old empire waned a great new infusion of virile barbarian life had come into Europe from the North and the East, and when some sort of social pattern began to emerge from the chaos of what Toynbee calls 'the sordid interlude between the death of one civilization and the birth of another', the imprint of the barbarians was unmistakably impressed upon it. It was an additional complication to the history of Christianity during this period that the Germanic tribes who poured in from the beleaguered fringes of the empire were themselves Christians, but their conversion had been at the hands of Arians, whose version of Christian doctrine was officially anathematized. In consequence, their coming, and their rapid domination of all aspects of society, including religion, made 'orthodoxy' both unorthodox and perilous, while it also added a racial and political element to the doctrinal controversies which shook the Church. It is hardly surprising that, in these circumstances, violence, superstition and intolerance became normal features of a nominally Christian society. The work of the Vandals in North Africa is the most obvious example of this brutalizing process. Gaiseric, and later his son Hunneric, were tyrants of the worst sort, and they exhibited their incredible cruelties to the world in the guise of outstanding zeal for Arian

Christianity. This barbarization of Christianity was not universal, of course, and there were quiet backwaters where saintly and scholarly men laid aside treasures of learning and piety which were later to become the inspiration of a more spacious age, but the vigour and unreason of Gothic peoples and their cult of personal authority left a permanent mark on the character of the Church, a Church which was to emerge as a dominant force in the new society.

Nor was it only barbarian vigour and love of authority which Europe carried forward to the formation of the new society of the middle ages. The hiatus left in post-classical society by the slow attrition of rationalism had been filled by an influx of superstition, emotionalism, and magic from the East. The later pagans, faced by the growing power of Christianity, resorted increasingly to claims of magical power. Concern for the salvation of the soul was general, and there was a good deal of sympathy for religious systems which claimed to provide salvation by initiation, or by the imparting of esoteric knowledge. This kind of religious irrationalism can generally win a good deal of popular support because its ethical demands are slight or non-existent, and it delivers its devotees from the exacting business of reconciling religion, nature, and society in one system of rational interpretation. A sense of wonder, a fund of readily-stimulated emotion, and an unlimited degree of credulity will together open this door of escape. Here, again, men are invited to surrender to authority, and to acknowledge the adept's claim to necessary but inexplicable knowledge and power. As the pagan survivals passed away, the task of providing this kind of religious satisfaction was accepted by the Christian Church. To some extent this process may be seen, and is so represented by some apologists, as a laudable sanctification of popular religious elements of undeniably pagan origin, but there was also a reciprocal process at work whereby pagan elements not only helped to shape the form of popular Christian devotion, but also entered deeply into the Christian conception of the ministry and the sacraments with consequences which still persist. This quasi-magical inheritance could not, however, be incorporated without a due claim to the unchallengeable and irrational authority which is its necessary counterpart. In such ways the weight of authority grew oppressively great. The conflation of circumstances was irresistible. Greek perspicacity and curiosity had been largely expunged from society by Roman love of authority and system. To the Roman mind it was more congenial to discuss the present shape of society than to question its origins and its fitness to meet the needs of men. Finally, the middle classes of the old empire, the bulwark of Roman democracy, disappeared almost entirely. 'In the enactments stretching from Constantine to Majorian which are included in the code of Justinian, we can trace, through a hundred and fifty years and 192 edicts, the slow destruction of the middle classes.'[9]

The society which began to emerge provided none of the conditions in which freedom of the mind and free intercourse of ideas can exist. Communication was broken by the fraction of society into isolated feudal units, and within those units the rule of the strong dominated every aspect of life. Moreover, communication with the wisdom of the past, and the refreshment of direction which comes from observing the mistakes and successes of former men and societies, were no longer accessible. The very considerable knowledge of the world which had been accumulated by the ancients was apparently lost. According to strict ecclesiastical reckoning, the whole corpus of heathen literature was heretical and philosophy, according to Tertullian, was the patriarch of the heresies. As a result, the middle ages were to inherit, by the direct route, only pitiful fragments of the ancient culture and wisdom. What survived, however, was enough to seed the new age. In the Church itself there were always some repositories in which the old learning could find sanctuary, so that when the desire for knowledge from a more spacious past was rekindled, it was not only from Moslem archives, but from the shabby obscurity of Italian and Irish monasteries, that the old voices were recovered. So Bacon was not entirely beside the mark when he claimed that 'It was the Christian church, which, amidst the inundations of the Scythians on the one side from the north-west, and the Saracens from the East, did preserve in the sacred lap and bosom thereof the precious relics even of heathen learning, which otherwise had been extinguished as if no such thing had ever been.'[10]

---

[9] Moss, op. cit., p. 29.
[10] *The Advancement of Learning* (World Classics Edn., Oxford), p. 45.

CHAPTER THREE

THE REVIVAL OF THE GREEK SPIRIT OF FREE ENQUIRY

THE FIRST movements toward a new era of intellectual freedom came from within the Church itself. Although so much trouble had been taken to establish the principle of authority at the expense of freedom, the Greek spirit was never quite extinct within the Church. During the ninth century the notion of authority was stiffened and codified, while new concepts of episcopal authority and of the supremacy of the Roman Pontiff were being adumbrated by Hincmar of Reims (d. 882), and added to the already formidable and acknowledged authority of the canonical scriptures, the Fathers, the great councils, and the tradition of the Church; but at the same time men like Johannes Scotus Erigena were recalling their contemporaries to a bolder use of critical reasoning. Indeed, it is difficult to say whether the incipient rationalism of the few was a reaction against the growing tendency to augment the power of authority, or whether the defences of authority were being strengthened to resist the nascent forces of freedom. A. J. Macdonald takes the latter view, that 'the rational attack of the Caroling era upon old ideas was responsible for a tightening of the standards of theological thought'.[1] John the Scot has been called the father of medieval rationalism,[2] but his rationalism was of the kind which provided a model for the rationalism of the scholastics. In other words, he did not seek to undermine Christian doctrine or the established authority of the Church, but exhibited an exuberant use of reason within the framework of professed orthodoxy. Scotus started from a conviction of the unity of truth. Both religion and philosophy, he reasoned, come ultimately from the wisdom of God and any incompatibility simply indicates an error on one side or the other. It follows that the Scriptures, though given by the authority of

[1] *Authority and Reason in the Early Middle Ages* (Oxford, 1933), p. 74.
[2] De Wolf, *History of Medieval Philosophy* (Nelson, English trans., 1952), I.124.

God, may be interpreted quite fearlessly by reason. If the result is indeed in accordance with reason it is thereby in conformity with authority. 'All authority which is not approved by true reason turns out to be weak. But true Reason, seeing that it stands firm and immutable, protected by its own virtues, needs not to be strengthened by any confirmation of Authority. True Authority, indeed, seems nothing but truth unified by the power of Reason, and transmitted in letters by the Holy Fathers for the benefit of posterity.'[3] Reason, for Erigena, was logically prior to authority, and once this is suspected to be the case, authority ceases to be unquestionable. It does not appear that the full extent of the danger to ecclesiastical authority which lay in the work of Erigena was fully realized at the time, for although Pope Nicholas I issued a faint rumble of protest and the Bishop of Lyons delivered a warning, *De Divisione Naturae* was not officially condemned to the flames until 1125.

As the scholastic movement grew in numbers and prestige, the name, but not the entire nature of philosophy, was restored; and while it is true that the Schoolmen were unduly occupied with dialectic and expended a great deal of their energy on the manipulation of terms, it was true at least that wits were being sharpened and men were being taught to ask questions and to place some reliance on ratiocination. The problem of Universals, which attracted so much attention in the middle ages, provided a fairly harmless area of disputation in which the sensation of debate could be enjoyed, with all the desirable consequences which attend a sound controversy, without matters of real importance to the Church and society suffering challenge. There was a concealed challenge, however, in the very vigour with which the debate was joined, and in the eagerness of so many restless minds to challenge orthodoxy, even if it was only on a matter where the salvation of the soul was not said to be at stake. Furthermore, even the subject of debate had a certain significance for the future. Nominalism is the obvious ally of Empiricism and its tendency is to steer men away from simple reliance on authority and from the tendency to generalize. 'A dogma is a past generalization which is divorced from the correcting influence of new facts and taken as necessarily and absolutely true. With such traditional generalizations the Church was identified: it stood for authority rather than

---

[3] Quoted by Lewes, *History of Philosophy* (London, 1880), II.11.

investigation—the authority of other people's experience of the past. To centre attention on the particular facts out of which generalizations grow, and to maintain the superior validity of these facts, was to substitute the principle of private judgement'.[4] It is significant, moreover, that those who held the doctrine of Realism in its extreme form came to be called '*antiqui doctores*', and that up to the end of the twelfth century the adversaries of this kind of realism were called '*moderni*'.[5]

Anselm of Canterbury was the other great figure of the period for whom the title 'Father of Scholasticism' has been claimed. From his work came the hope of a leavening of authority itself with new ideas. In the circumstances of the time it was unlikely that freedom would be attained in one leap. Nor is it certain that those who challenged authority directly were in fact responsible for the most significant changes in the old order. Anselm worked unobtrusively and kept the respect and esteem of his fellows, but he succeeded in gaining acceptance for the application of the dialectical method to questions of dogma. He was also responsible for some of the first Christian essays in natural theology, and whatever absolute value there may or may not be in natural theology, the very fact that his contemporaries were led to accept the legitimacy of intellectual inquiry in a field which touched the dogmas of the Church, meant a relaxation, however insensible, of the theological absolutism of the past. For a time, at least, more room was to be left for the operation of the intellect. Even though the enclosing barriers of doctrinal definition were as rigid as ever, they receded somewhat to allow the inquiring mind a freer play, and it has been suggested that this increased freedom, whereby 'the dialectical method and rational enquiry were permanently established in theological disquisition', was in some degree a result of the writings of Anselm.[6]

Progress, however, was checked from time to time by the understandable fears of a more conservative point of view which saw in the increasing use of reason the doom of the age of faith, and feared that this incessant probing would destroy the foundation of authority upon which medieval society had been firmly established. Hence the whole period of the middle ages is one of mental and spiritual unrest and struggle, and the Renaissance is the

---

[4] Rogers, *Students' History of Philosophy* (New York, 1932), p. 195.
[5] De Wolf, op. cit., p. 143.   [6] Macdonald, op. cit., p. 90.

culmination of a long process of growth and development. An instance of the kind of check in progress which we have in mind is afforded by the later stages of the eucharistic controversy between Berengar (whose teaching was ultimately to be condemned with that of Erigena in 1050) and Lanfranc. Lanfranc was eager enough to engage in controversy and to fight Berengar with his chosen weapon of dialectic. But when the fight began to get out of hand, and when doctrines which to Lanfranc were immutable Catholic truth seemed to be imperilled by the readier wit of his adversary, he looked about for another weapon. 'The readiest to hand was the hardening theory of ecclesiastical authority, the use of scriptural and patristic passages as proof-texts, which did not admit of discussion, still less of debate, and which were being wielded—like the Conqueror's mace—to crash through the skilful sword-play of dialectics, in order to bring down an opponent at a blow' (ibid., p. 94).

The Carolignian renaissance had provided a glimpse of freedom; a freedom made possible by the slightly relaxed authority of the Frankish kings. But the time soon came when the trial of strength between the Empire and the Papacy was to show a balance in favour of the Papacy. Absolute authority which has been acquired by the sword need not be rigorous except where the right to command obedience is directly challenged, but absolute authority which is claimed by a plea of moral and spiritual inerrancy cannot afford to be so accommodating. Nevertheless, an uneasy compromise was established. The new taste for dialectics persisted, however we may smile at the rather limited material with which it was usually allowed to work; and, from time to time, there is evinced an independence of judgement and a boldness of utterance which would not have disgraced the Athens of a former day. As an example of this we may cite the case of the anonymous Yorkist whose writings date from the end of the eleventh century and the beginning of the twelfth.[7] The Yorkist attacked clerical celibacy and the conception of a universal Church under Roman hegemony. He disputed the power of the Pope to create new ecclesiastical laws or to issue doctrinal definitions. 'The authority for the Christian in morals and belief lies in the Gospels and Epistles. The Pope has no higher jurisdiction than any other bishop. . . . There are two churches at Rome, one

---

[7] See Macdonald, ibid., pp. 114ff.

of Satan and one of Christ, and the membership of the latter is small.' (ibid., pp. 119-20).

This voice of revolt was never silent in the years that followed. Restraints upon freedom were multiplied, but it is often forgotten that this was itself a measure of the increasing intellectual restlessness within Christendom. So difficult was it to divert the impetus of the new dialectical tendency that the method was to some extent taken over by authority and used to reinforce its own position. Hence by degrees the use of reason in theological discourse became respectable, though it was required of reason so employed that it should operate without disturbing unduly the authority of scripture and tradition. It is clear, however, that the dialectical phase was not in vain. The skills, aptitudes, and interests which had arisen from a preoccupation with the technicalities and applications of Aristotelian logic were not likely to be satisfied for very long with the materials offered by the careful hand of the Church, so that when the exiled treasures of Greek thought began to creep back into Christendom, dusty and a little damaged by the long Arabian night, many keen, unsatisfied minds were waiting to welcome them. Some of these, like Aquinas, were understandably dominated by their theological interests and were delighted at the prospect of an enlarged and rationalized, and yet perfectly Christian, philosophy. In their hands Aristotle became a sound churchman, fitted exactly into his strange new niche by the careful labours of his commentators.

Roger Bacon, too, was firmly attached to the usual theological anchors, but the effect of the current of new ideas was quite different in his case. It was not his primary concern to give a new rational articulation to the old doctrine, but to direct men to the source of new knowledge. To that end he advocated the use of observation and experiment in terms which suggest an outlook very much in advance of his age. But although he realized that any useful knowledge of nature must depend upon the employment of an independent and unhampered technique of investigation, he did not subscribe to the notion that theological truth and philosophical truth belong to different orders of reality. This conception of the relationship between the authoritative pronouncements of scripture, on the one hand, and the speculations of philosophy, on the other, had been seized upon with delight by those of his contemporaries who felt themselves to be in danger of flying too close to the brink of heresy. Against this point of view, which he regarded as itself heretical, Bacon insisted upon the unity of truth, and the consequent interconnexion of all intellectual disciplines. We now regard this as the right point of view, but in the period which followed Bacon the Church was in two minds about it. If she regarded matters of science as distinct from the truth declared by scripture and tradition, then new discoveries could be assimilated without any serious modification of her teaching and without the sacrifice of her intellectual primacy. But this course, which promised so well, afforded too much latitude to the speculative, and when the volume of new ideas became sufficiently great an irresistible challenge to the authority of the Church developed.

This was the situation to which the Renaissance brought its bewildering assortment of new ideas from the golden past and its hitherto undreamed-of aspirations for the future. Although the Church herself was fascinated by the new treasures of learning, she was not able to assimilate them in any way which could prevent the growth of a new empire of secular knowledge. The dimmed lights of Constantinople were at last extinguished by the Turks, but from the gloom of her ending her quiet scholars came out to the light of Italy and brought with them their disturbing burden of classical learning. At last the enlightenment of which a few men had dreamed at their peril became the open inheritance of a new civilization. There was a new and passionate regard for the glories of the ancient world and a hunger for the wisdom of her sages. A revival of interest in the arts and literature would not have been of first-class importance had it remained merely antiquarian in interest, however great the reverence and understanding with which it looked to the past. Antiquarianism, however, was only the stimulus and pattern which, in the arts, gave rise to a great surge of creative feeling and activity which transformed the aesthetic life of Europe; while in the field of religion it produced not only a challenge to authority characteristic of the new impulse to freedom, but a marked tendency to revert to the antique and venerable origins of the Christian faith and to discard at least some of the superstitious accretions of the centuries. In philosophy also, there was much more to be gained than a revived interest in the past. A juster assessment of the teaching of Aristotle and a first clear view of Plato's wide territory were both valuable gains, but still more valuable was the stimulus that men received to think for themselves and to rebel against all manner of dogmatic imposition. We come here to the brink of the modern era in philosophy, and there is no better representative of the phase of transition, and no sturdier protagonist of intellectual freedom, than Giordano Bruno (d. 1600). For Bruno, all authority was suspect, and the restraining hand of the past was as irksome to him as the prejudice and ignorance of those of his contemporaries who still preferred to settle intellectual disputes with a thumbscrew and a bonfire. Bruno was destroyed by the Roman Church, or by the State, if we are inclined to take notice of the shabby fiction which was supposed to free the Pope from the guilt of executions even when it was he who required that they should be carried out. Others were to follow, victims of both Catholic and Protestant bigotry and intolerance. But at last the whole idea of authority was facing a challenge. The long story of intellectual and religious persecution is still a horror and a disturbance to us. It may be pleaded in mitigation of the cruelties that were perpetrated that brutality and violence were characteristic aspects of medieval life, and that the whole period was one of extreme emotional instability. Life 'bore the mixed smell of blood and roses. The men of that time always oscillated between the fear of hell and the most naïve joy, between cruelty and tenderness, between harsh asceticism and insane attachment to the delights of this world, between hatred and goodness, always running to extremes'.[8] But we must be reluctant to blame the emotional and moral condition of the people, when the society which nurtured them had been shaped and determined, to a very great extent, by an authority which insisted that it was beyond their control. Persecution could not have become a dominant and regulative force had men not come to believe that the immutable truth had been entrusted to an organization in perpetuity, and had it not therefore seemed that the safety of Church and Empire, and therefore of home and family, depended upon a resolute defence of the *status quo*. Once it became possible for enough men to see that the domain of the true is infinitely extensible and open to the inquiry of all men, the old world was under notice of dismissal and the new world was at the door.

[8] J. Huizinga, *The Waning of the Middle Ages* (Penguin edn., 1955), pp. 26f.

CHAPTER FOUR

THE MODERN CONFLICT TAKING SHAPE—THE PLACE OF AUTHORITY IN THE DEVELOPMENT OF MODERN THOUGHT

WHILST the Renaissance and the Reformation together provided much of the impetus which drove men forward to the new age of reason and discovery, the force was indirectly applied. In both cases there was a partial satisfaction of men's need to acquire knowledge and to renovate the organs of learning and the institutions of society. But in each case there was the hint of the emergence of a new authority. The Renaissance had acted as a powerful stimulant of new ideas, but it had also laid upon Europe the heavy hand of ancient tradition and fathered a whole race of scholars whose ingenuity was for the most part expended upon commentary, correlation and analysis. The past had been for a long time neglected, now it was enthroned. The Reformation promised religious freedom, but it failed at its first attempt to do much more than divide the religious world into a number of domains, each of which continued to exercise a more or less excessive degree of authority. From the point of view of the philosopher, a world of conflicting authorities is likely to provide more room for individual points of view than a world where authority has been firmly placed in one strong centre. But the stage of conflict is inherently imperfect and is likely to move towards the unreal freedom of complete scepticism or to lapse into a modified authoritarianism either by way of syncretism or absorption.

It is fairly clear that since the beginning of the seventeenth century movements of both kinds have taken place. The old, uneasy equilibrium of medieval theocracy was succeeded by a time of divided rule. Western civilization broke into irregular national segments, and the influence of nationalism became apparent, not only in the political field, but in religion and philosophy too. The nationality of Augustine or St Thomas Aquinas is of very little interest to us, and the same could probably be said of Erigena, or Anselm, or Abelard. But it is much more difficult to forget the German background of Kant and Hegel and Nietzsche, or the Englishness of Locke and Mill (though one must be careful here; the more impressively English philosophers turn out to be Scots or Irishmen). Nationalism, however, had something to offer scientists and philosophers, if it was only the assurance that most of their enemies would be abroad. Giordano Bruno tasted this security in Elizabethan England but he chose to move on into the restless uncertainties of Europe rather than expose his mind to the perils of Oxford rusticity. Francis Bacon, on the other hand, was happy enough to be at home in the peace of England. Although some kind of rebellion against authority is implicit in his work as a philosopher, he was no rebel by nature, but a careful and accomplished courtier. It is Bacon's attitude to religious authority that we shall examine now since, whatever his technical limitations as a philosopher, it was the broad sweep of his mind which first envisaged the possible extent and usefulness of scientific knowledge.

Bacon's obvious respect for royal authority, and the obsequious tone of some of his references to King James, may have harmed his reputation among more rebellious spirits, but statesmanship was his job, and its necessary gestures must not be credited with an undue amount of meaning. It is obvious that his courtly word often had a philosophical purpose, for the advancement of the 'new method' was the bounty which he really hoped for from his king. With regard to spiritual authority, it seems to have been commonly understood that Bacon spoke with his tongue in his cheek, anxious to preserve the appearance of orthodoxy in order to keep on the right side of the Church—and the throne. It may be true that he 'emphasized in *De Augmentis* his authoritarian theology' in order 'to guard himself after his keen thrusts in the *Novum Organon* at theological hindrances to the sciences',[1] but it is even more likely that Bacon was perfectly sincere in his references to theology. It must be remembered that medieval thinkers had established the utility of the doctrine of 'twofold truth', and had found in it a means of liberating their secular thinking without exposing themselves to the charge of theological error. Why is there any difficulty in supposing that Bacon accepted the elbow room which this doctrine provided with the conviction that he

[1] J. M. Robertson, in his introduction to Bacon's *Philosophical Works*, annotated by Ellis and Spedding (Routledge, 1905).

was neither intellectually inconsistent nor impious? 'This likewise I humbly pray, that things human may not interfere with things divine, and that from the opening of the ways of sense and the increase of natural light there may arise in our minds no incredulity or darkness with regard to the divine mysteries: but rather that the understanding being thereby purified and purged of fancies and vanity, and yet not the less subject and entirely submissive to the divine oracles, may give to faith that which is faith's.'[2] He was concerned to call men to an unprejudiced and methodical study of the natural world and it was his belief that they would find nothing there to upset their theology. Adam was punished not for seeking knowledge, but for seeking God's own knowledge, the knowledge of good and evil (ibid., p. 61). It is clear from what follows that Bacon would not have recommended the application of the inductive method to ethics, since he believed that ethics rested upon the original command of God. If he did not think it possible to apply the results of scientific observation to theology, it was not because he was afraid of the consequences, but because he was Platonist enough to believe that natural phenomena conceal God rather than reveal Him (cf. ibid., p. 247). By this he does not intend to assert that nature has nothing to say about God, for he would have had no difficulty in accepting Berkeley's concept of nature as 'a divine visual language', but, in his view, what the contemplation of nature brings to our quest for the divine is a sense of wonder and not knowledge (*Valerius Terminus*, ibid., p. 186). Therefore the Christian philosopher can, in Bacon's view, apply himself to the business of natural philosophy with complete freedom and at the same time 'give unto faith that which unto faith belongeth: for more worthy is it to believe than to think or know' (ibid., p. 187). Perhaps the truth behind all this is quite simple. Bacon did not need to be hypocritical in his references to religious authority. He was glad enough to be rid of ultimate questions. He was neither a theologian nor a metaphysician but the herald of a new attitude to the facts of the human environment. From this point of view it was a wholly admirable circumstance if matters beyond the scope of his method could be regarded as settled. His sincerity in this seems to me to be indicated in his strictures on religion which 'consisteth in rites and forms of adoration, and not in confessions

[2] From the preface to *The Great Instauration, Philosophical Works*, pp. 246f.

of belief.' (ibid., p. 204). Such a religion, according to Bacon, tempts men to mingle science with theology in a way which is detrimental to discovery. Each discipline must refer to its own proper authority, for a mixing of the two will make 'an heretical religion and an imaginary and fabulous philosophy'. (*Advancement of Learning*, ibid., p. 92). Bacon seemed to find in the reformed Church of England exactly the kind of religious authority which was agreeable to him, not leaving too much to wasteful argument, as the Greeks had done to the detriment of their practical science, or interdicting argument altogether as Islam did (ibid., p. 169).

The emphasis in Bacon's attitude to religion was very much like that which characterized his approach to science. For him the great matter, the business which nearly concluded research, was to record the facts. A sufficiently thorough process of sifting and classification would then enable the most ordinary man to make signal discoveries and to advance the lot of his fellows in a corresponding degree. Now in science, the facts are apprehended by simple observation, but in religion, according to his idea of the matter, the facts are wholly given by God in revelation, and man's reason may then be used to interpret and relate the facts. Since, given the true facts, the scientist cannot go far wrong, it would follow that the theologian, whose facts are provided by authority, has an almost foolproof task. The laws of the game are laid down and he has only to determine the tactics; or, to change the figure, the court has rules of justice which are '*placita juris*, positive upon authority, and not upon reason, and therefore not to be disputed: but what is most just, not absolutely but relatively, and according to those maxims, that affordeth a long field of disputation. Such therefore is that secondary reason which hath place in divinity, which is grounded upon the "placets" of God' (ibid., p. 169).

Bacon was insistent, however, that religious scruples should not in any circumstances be permitted to inhibit the investigation of nature's secrets. To fasten religious doctrines to particular philosophical systems was to bring harm both to religion and philosophy, as was clear from the fate of the Christian thinkers who had committed themselves to an Aristotelian view of the world. Nor must investigation be deterred by the fear that 'it may lead to an innovation in divinity, or else should discover matter of further contradiction to divinity' (*Filum Labyrinthi*, ibid., p. 209). He has the very strongest distaste for the kind of religious dogmatism which inspires furious controversy about matters which are intrinsically uncertain. In such debates he recommends the style of Paul, who offered a dubious theological opinion as '*ego, non dominus*'. 'But men are now over-ready to usurp the style, *non ego, sed dominus*' (ibid., p. 170).

While Bacon thus sought to disengage himself, rather carefully, from the authority of the Church, he was much more radical in his attitude to the authority of tradition. A long period of respect for the learning of antiquity, as well as the virtual beatification of Aristotle by the Church, had left men with a distrust of their own wits. Bacon had little patience with this slavish attitude to the old learning. Surely in most practical matters, he reasoned, it is clear that time has brought knowledge and progress. 'Artillery, sailing, printing, and the like, were grossly mismanaged at the first, and by time accommodated and refined, whereas the vigorous science and philosophy of the ancients has become emaciated. Surely this is because practical skills are developed by the contribution of the skill and experience of many men, whereas in science, as it has hitherto been understood, the many have relied on the few' (ibid., p. 58). If we depend on Aristotle for our knowledge we shall never know more than Aristotle. Bacon denominates this undue reliance on authority as a disease of learning, but on closer examination it appears that all three of his 'diseases of learning' are the effects of a too-credulous attitude to authority. If reverence for antiquity seduces men to this error they should realize that we are the true antiquity. The ancients belong to the youth of learning and 'for its value and utility it must be plainly avowed that that wisdom which we have derived principally from the Greeks is but the boyhood of knowledge' (Preface to *The Great Instauration*, ibid., p. 243). But men are still prone to believe that all the worth-while discoveries must have been made already and that novelty will always turn out, upon closer examination, to be error which has already been rejected. This artificial power of the past to dominate men's minds may be due in part to the dogmatic tone in which tradition is handed down; a fault which may be rectified by abandoning the 'magistral and peremptory' manner and by 'propounding things sincerely, with more or less asseveration, as they stand in a man's own judgement proved more or less' (ibid., p. 60). It is true that Aristotle went to the other extreme and disregarded the gains of the past altogether in his anxiety to be novel (ibid., p. 92), but, on the whole, error is more likely to lie in the other direction, for 'Time is like a river, which has brought down to us things light and puffed up, while those which are weighty and solid have sunk' (Preface to *The Great Instauration*, ibid., p. 244).

Since Bacon sought to limit the territory over which the Church could claim authority, and shook off many of the restraints exercised by tradition, we might expect to find him advancing some new sources of authority. In view of his predilection for the inductive method we might expect a reference to 'the authority of the facts', but Bacon was less modern than that, and possibly more careful to keep in view the reciprocal processes which are always involved in knowing: there can be no authority in facts unless they are reliably observed and recorded. The sub-heading of the preface of *The Great Instauration* speaks of the need to open a way for the understanding 'entirely different from any hitherto known, and other helps provided, in order that the mind may exercise over the nature of things the authority which properly belongs to it' (ibid., p. 243). This is to be done, oddly enough, by keeping so close to nature that the facts will be seen to be related with the least possible intervention of the intelligence. So little is contributed by the investigator that 'strength and excellency of the wit' no longer count for very much, and the very senses by means of which we come by our perceptions of nature are suspect, and can only be trusted if we employ a method which assists their operation and compensates for their aberrations.

It is perhaps fair to conclude that although Bacon did not know exactly where his authority was to be found, he did know where it was not to be found. The kind of scientific authority which he sought to establish was not to be reached, however, by a deductive delineation of the advantages of the inductive method, but only by the increasing confidence which springs from the results of a prodigious amount of practical work and the methodical assessment of failures and successes over a long period.

*   *   *

The solution offered to the problem of authority by Thomas Hobbes had the great merit of simplicity and clarity. Like Descartes, Hobbes believed that beneath the complex surface pattern of the world lay purely mechanical processes; but he admitted only bodies and notion into his scheme, for he excluded the Cartesian notion of an independent mind-substance and regarded the operation of the mind as nothing more than internal motion. He conceived a world devoid of Aristotelian final causes and freed from all manner of mysterious and distance-bridging forces; a world in which all operations, whether mental or physical, were the result of contacts between bodies or parts of bodies and of the exchange of motion consequent upon such contacts. Working from the bottom upwards, he defined man in terms of the animal kingdom and was satisfied to account for his behaviour in terms of a more or less modified operation of instinctive tendencies to self-preservation. If living organisms of this character are set over against one another in relative isolation, they must lapse into a state of mutual hostility in which there can be no victory; for the condition of any man whom we may choose to consider is that of solitariness, for which there is no help, and which must expect to find itself on the losing side when its very existence is a threat to the welfare of more numerous competitors. This, fortunately, does not constitute a complete deadlock in the human situation. Just as the simple elements of the non-human world develop a highly complex universe from their mutual motion, so effects of great complexity and subtlety are produced in the affairs of men by means of simple egoistic causes which are the mainsprings of human behaviour. By this means man is driven towards the establishment of the State, a system of authority in which the individual can find the greatest chance of security and satisfaction.

This is the simple basis of the view of the State outlined by Hobbes. Men come to an arrangement with a sovereign whereby he is permitted to exercise complete authority. But since the motive for the creation of his authority is the protection of the individual, this protective function must be the aim and end of the State, and the individual is only bound to observe its authority so long as he receives protection. A man may have outstanding gifts of leadership and understanding, like Plato's philosopher-king, but no authority may be ascribed to him on that account. The authority of the king, who is the embodiment of the State, is a conditional surrender of the natural rights of his people. The king is not the rightful father of his people by virtue of his noble birth, the people are really the fathers of the king, because their surrendered rights are the foundation of his authority.

Hobbes rejects the notion that an appeal to the authority of God, as one might appeal to a higher court, may by-pass the authority of the sovereign. For practical purposes the king is the final authority in matters of religion as in secular affairs: 'There is no Covenant with God, but by the mediation of some body that representeth God's person; which none doth but God's Lieutenant, who hath the Sovereignty under God'.[3] There is therefore no loophole for the aspiring Puritan who wishes to appeal to a higher authority. Even Holy Scripture, so far as it has mandatory force, comes to us on the authority of the sovereign, and he is its supreme interpreter (ibid., p. 210). There can be no conflicting loyalties in a scheme of natural authority, so that a system of dual control by Church and State is out of the question. It seems that the old error was to dissociate the Church from the State whereas, in Hobbes' scheme, the commonwealth is a Christian commonwealth indistinguishable from what the Church ought to be. It has already been argued that there is no authority in a multiplicity of persons, but only in one person, and since the spiritual realm appears to coincide with the temporal, and in any case there cannot be two authorities or there would be none, it follows that the spiritual head we are seeking is the same as the temporal head, the sovereign himself (ibid., p. 209). He is the only authoritative teacher of his people, from whom subordinate teachers derive their licence (ibid., p. 127), and his moral authority is supreme, so that a private citizen may not appeal to his own conscience about any matter in which he is called to obey the sovereign (ibid., p. 172). The vexed question of ecclesiastical authority is settled quite easily. The effective power in religion is the king's, and the Church quite properly has no power to command but only licence to proclaim a kingdom which is not yet realized. In other words, the Church's sovereignty is in the future, while the monarch's sovereignty is a present necessity (ibid., pp. 268-70). In the meantime the authority of the ministry itself rests upon the sovereign 'to whose charge the whole flock of his subjects is committed', and it is by his authority 'that all other Pastors are made, and have power to teach, and perform all other pastoral offices'. The clergy are, in fact, ministers of the crown (ibid., p. 294).

The system outlined by Hobbes may seem to us now to be such a monstrous concatenation of perilous fallacies that we are

---

[3] *Leviathan* (Everyman Edn., p. 91).

affected by it as he himself was by the mysteries of religion, which he described as 'wholesome pills for the sick, which swallowed whole, have the vertue to cure; but chewed, are for the most part cast up without effect' (ibid., p. 199). But that is not to say that Hobbes erected a purely artificial authority to bring unnatural order into a naturally 'brutish' and disordered world. It may be perfectly true that the model of contract was 'a device which gave expression to a shift in attitude toward authority', an attempt to substitute legal-rational authority for patriarchalism,[4] but it is doubtful whether, for Hobbes, it was a conscious device. We must give him some credit for being misguided, and be prepared to allow for his complete trust in egoistic premisses and the deductive method. He himself was quite satisfied that he had reasoned in the only correct way from man's primitive natural state to the society which fitted his condition and met all his needs: 'I have derived the Rights of Sovereign Power, and the duty of Subjects hitherto, from the Principles of Nature only; such as experience has found true, or Consent (concerning the use of words) has made so; that is to say from the nature of Men known to us by Experience, and from Definitions (of such words as are Essential to all Political reasoning) universally agreed on'.[5] It is with Hobbes's version of the 'principles of nature' that we must quarrel, and especially we must doubt whether a hypothetical human condition of isolation and complete egoism ever represented more than the unhappy lot of a few abnormal and unacceptable members of the primitive family circle. And it is clear as Sorley has put it,[6] that 'when we recognize that the individual is neither real nor intelligible apart from his social origin and traditions, and that the social factor influences his thoughts and motives, the opposition between self and others becomes less fundamental, the abrupt alternatives of Hobbism lose their validity, and it is possible to regard morality and the State as expressing the ideal and sphere of human activity, and not as simply the chains by which man's unruly passions are kept in check'.

* * *

Like Bacon, Descartes realized how much men needed to escape from the dominion of the past and from an uncritical acceptance

---

[4] Richard Peters, *Hobbes* (Pelican Books, 1956), p. 198.   [5] *Leviathan*, p. 199.
[6] In his *History of English Philosophy* (Cambridge, 1920), p. 69.

of their own prejudices and ill-founded judgements. The starting-point which he proposed to himself was 'a mind so far withdrawn from corporeal things that it does not even know that anyone has existed before it, and hence cannot be influenced by the authority of others'.[7] This is obviously an exaggeration, for no educated man can entirely insulate himself from the past. But Descartes made the effort, not by pretending that the past could be ignored, but by treating the wisdom of the past as a field of observation, so that for him, 'to hold converse with those of other ages and to travel, are almost the same thing'.[8] In any case it is arguable that Descartes' own success or failure to achieve detachment is less important than his success in impressing the need for detachment on his philosophical contemporaries and successors; for in the new fashion of philosophizing 'that reverence for hard words and dark notions by which men's understanding had been strangled in earlier years, was turned into contempt, and everything suspected which was not clearly and distinctly understood'.[9] We shall see that Reid's estimate is somewhat too generous, but the broad sense of it is just. Descartes did not seem to feel that '*reculer pour mieux sauter*' was a sound maxim for philosophers; rather did he insist that to move backwards at all is always to delay progress, and that 'they who have learned the least of all that has been hitherto distinguished by the name of philosophy are the most fitted for the apprehension of truth'.[10] This is the point at which it is most convenient for us to fix the beginning of modern philosophy and, although all such beginnings are arbitrarily conceived, as Leibniz pointed out a little later, there is at least no more obvious starting-point, and no more clearly reasoned attempt to detach the whole field of speculation from the authoritarian trammels of the middle ages.

The authority of the past, so far as it was external, could be dealt with by a deliberate act of disengagement, but it was not so easy to deal with the consequences of tradition which had already attached themselves to our own idiosyncrasies to form prejudices that were internal to the thinking subject. This situation was met by Descartes by the method of doubt. By this means he sought to whittle away all preconceived ideas except those which would

[7] *Reply to Gassendi* (Scribner's Edn.), p. 251.
[8] *Discourse* (Blackwood, 1925), p. 7.
[9] Reid, *Essays on the Intellectual Powers of Man*, ed. Woozley (Macmillan, 1941), p. 98.
[10] Preface to the *Principles*, p. 179.

stand the test of 'clarity and distinctness'. This test itself was rigorous enough as Descartes employed it, but its subjective character made it a variable and imprecise criterion of truth. Yet somewhere here lay the new seat of authority which Descartes was trying to find. Since authority was not to be conceded to declarations handed down from the past, a new basis of certainty must be uncovered by the removal of all the encumbering layers of uncertainty. 'Archimedes, that he might transport the entire globe from the place it occupied to another, demanded only a point that was firm and immovable; so also, I shall be entitled to entertain the highest expectations, if I am fortunate enough to discover only one thing that is certain and indubitable.'[11] He succeeded in finding, to his own satisfaction, more than one such principle, for it is erroneous to suppose that all that followed was deduced from the fundamental *'cogito ergo sum'*. This was a primary principle, but there were other and parallel innate ideas on which Descartes placed reliance. Consciousness did indeed possess its own power to certify selfhood but only because, so he felt, activity must be grounded in a subject; and this proposition, in turn, one would judge to have rested upon the principle of contradiction. For Descartes, with his mechanistic view of the world, 'to be' was 'to be a part of', and 'to be a part of' was to act. Put another way, so necessary was the connexion between action and substance that to acknowledge, 'there is thinking' and to doubt the thinker is to affirm and then to deny what is virtually the same proposition.

The existence of God was established, again to Descartes' own satisfaction, by a similar appeal, however covert, to the principle of contradiction. An effect has no greater reality than its cause, so his own conception of an infinite God must have an infinite cause. Again, the single step from activity to subject is taken, in what he thinks is the only appropriate direction, but since he assumes that qualities can only exist in a substance, the final appeal is simply to the proposition that it is fallacious to doubt the existence of an eternal God because his conception is an effect of his substance. The proposition, 'there is no eternal God', is self-contradictory in the sense in which 'There is none of this rain which is wetting my face' would be contradictory. It would seem that this concealed dependence upon the principle of contradiction might lend

[11] *Meditation* 2 (Edn. Veitch), p. 104.

plausibility to a good many statements which may be true or untrue, but are not necessarily so.

When we classify Descartes as a rationalist and call Bacon the father of Empiricism we are apt to be confounded by the complexity in simplicity which all great philosophy exhibits. Descartes would have argued that his method of doubt was empirical, and that it was only by a thoroughgoing empiricism that he ever reached the principles which then enabled him to generalize about the world. Even when this stage was passed, he was much more of a practical empiricist than Bacon himself so far as the particular sciences were concerned. It is therefore an oversimplification to say that Bacon sought the authority of the facts, or advocated such a course, while Descartes relied upon the authority inherent in the rationality of the human mind. Nevertheless it is true that, in the broadest sense, Descartes represents the tendency to look within and Bacon the objective, positivist tendency which prefers to ignore, as far as possible, the relation of the self to the process of observation and to the facts which are said to be observed. It is still a problem of some intricacy to determine whether the ultimate authorization of our knowledge of the world is to be found in the external data which we observe and collate, or whether the observing self is always in need of some guarantee, some authentification which, in the nature of the case, can only be self-authentification. That, however, is a topic for a later stage.

Descartes' attitude to external authority, and particularly to the authority of the Roman Church, was anything but robust. There can be no doubt that he was a sincerely religious man. For him, the difficult passage from the self to the phenomenal world was to be accomplished only by the help of God. God was the ultimate basis of his authority, because it was God who guaranteed the coherence of the experience of the self, and whose nature ruled out the hypothesis of self-delusion. Consciousness reveals selfhood, and finite selfhood carries within it the implication of an infinite God, and God then guarantees the validity of the subsequent operations of the self in its intercourse with the world. Without his reliance upon God there would have been a large gap in his system, but there is a candour and simplicity in the personality of Descartes which make it difficult to believe that God was only brought in to fill the gap. If he was sincere in this, however, it is almost impossible to believe that he was sincere in his submissive attitude to the authority of the Church. The ground of absolute certainty is the supreme goodness of God,[12] but it is still necessary for Descartes to submit all his opinions to the authority of the Church.[13] The former point, that certitude is based on the nature of God, is stated even more explicitly in CCVI; so that although God is vital to his system, he quietly hands over the whole domain of the knowledge of God to revelation, and exempts theology from rational examination.[14] He is well aware that the argument from the authority of scripture alone proceeds in a circle, the Scriptures being understood as guaranteed by God and then claimed to be the unique revelation of God; and he explains in the dedication to the *Meditations*[15] that for the benefit of infidels some rational intrusion into the circle is a necessary part of Christian apologetic. He goes on to suggest that such a break into the circle may be achieved by his method of doubt and introspection, but the certainty he has achieved he purports to lay at the feet of the Catholic professors of the Sorbonne in order to receive the authority of their approbation (ibid., p. 85). Now we may rest our certainties upon clear and distinct perception or we may submit to the judgement of other men; but we can hardly rely on both methods at the same time. This Descartes pretended to do, and it would be easy to tax him with insincerity on this account. Perhaps, however, it was only common sense for one who uttered a little heresy from time to time and even suggested that it was improbable that all things were made for the sake of man, to secure himself by a few saving clauses. Galileo was not so very long dead.

We must, however, be careful to distinguish the sense in which Descartes was prepared to concede authority in practical matters, in a more or less experimental fashion, so that the practical affairs of life need not be too much disturbed by philosophical doubt. It will be remembered that he accepted a practical ethical rule of this sort to tide him over the period when his uncertainty was greatest. In terms of his own metaphor, he needed a house to live in during the time when his own judgement was suspended,[16] and with this in view he determined to follow a few clear maxims

---

[12] *Principles*, XXIX, XXX.
[14] *Discourse on Method*, p. 9.
[16] *Discourse*, Part III.

[13] *Principles*, CCVII.
[15] Edn. Veitch, p. 82.

of his own devising. He resolved, for instance, to obey the laws and customs of his country, to persist in his adherence to the Christian faith, and to be positive and decided in his actions. This was not only a recipe for a quiet life, but a testimony to his own conviction that many of the affairs of life are adequately known by common sense; and that a virtual certainty existed on matters of observation which was a sufficient guide for practical affairs. It seems likely, therefore, that he regarded speculative freedom concerning philosophical problems as perfectly compatible with submission and conformity in practical affairs. Moreover, it is possible that we ought to regard his submission to the authority of the Church in this sense.

* * *

Leibniz, unlike either Bacon or Descartes, had no wish to detach himself from the thinkers of the past. Instead, he rejoiced in the extent of his philosophical inheritance, and though he never made the mistake of allowing undue reverence for tradition to blunt his criticism even of Plato and Aristotle, for whom he had much respect, he was anxious to learn from any source where truth might be discovered. Leibniz could no more accept the possibility of a philosophical clean sheet than he could allow that the mind might start from Locke's *'tabula rasa'*. 'Thought does not proceed *per saltum*. In the history of thinking, as in all other history, "the present is laden with the past and full of the future".'[17] His preoccupation with the notion of continuity made him welcome the contributions of his predecessors and try to understand in what sense they could be fitted into the general pattern of truth. Yet the only authority he recognized in the philosophy of the past was the authority of truth so far as it was present there. He was not impressed by the cult of names or the philosophical recommendations of the Church, but he delighted to find the thought of other men in substantial accord with his own conclusions, or to realize how his own ideas had developed from the suggestions of the past (and this is a fairly rare virtue).

This inclination to take orthodoxy seriously may have wasted Leibniz a good deal of time, as in the case of his attempt to reconcile Protestant and Catholic sacramental theology, or his patient, apologetic endeavours to convince M. Arnauld that he was not a

[17] Latta, in *The Monadology* (Oxford, 1898), p. 153.

heretic so far as his philosophy was concerned. Yet not all his respect for the past, or his undoubted reverence for the great men of the Roman Church could induce him to capitulate before its theological assaults upon freedom of thought. He was no more anxious than Descartes to bear the dark name of heresy, and even if he was somewhat less timid and the times were growing more favourable, he was still uneasy when he felt that his own speculations were driving him further and further away from his Roman friends. We may never know the true extent of his own uncertainty and conflict about this matter. There is a passage in a letter from Arnauld to Count Hessen-Rheinfels in which Arnauld indicates that the Count had already brought Leibniz to admit the claim of Rome to be the true Church. In the margin, Leibniz has written: 'I have never endorsed this sentiment.'[18] This is one incident from which Leibniz seems to emerge staunchly Protestant. Another aspect is noticeable in a letter from Leibniz to Hessen-Rheinfels dated 30th April 1687, in which Leibniz is anxious that his correspondent shall obtain from Arnauld an opinion about the degree and kind of error which may be incorporated in Leibniz' system. 'He is very busy' writes Leibniz, 'and his time is too valuable for me to pretend that he should employ it in discussing a matter regarding truth or falsehood of an opinion; but it is easy for him to decide upon its tolerability, since it is merely a question of knowing whether they are contrary to certain definitions of the Church' (ibid., pp. 200-1). 'They' refers to the theologically irregular opinions of the Molinists, whose degree of deviation Leibniz considers about equal to his own. His anxiety here is lest he should be guilty of impermissible error. It is difficult to see of what assistance Arnauld's assurance would have been. Yet it is evidence that Leibniz was prepared to treat the Roman Church with a careful respect, and this is perfectly in accord with his ambition to fit the present to the past and to show that his metaphysical discoveries were literally innovations, since they renewed the thought of the past and fulfilled the law without abolishing it. From Arnauld's point of view this was an unsatisfactory attitude, for Rome's theological norm was more rigid than Leibniz imagined, and although she allowed some latitude to her own philosophers, Arnauld was probably right to sense a fatal objection which she would have brought against 'the new system';

[18] *Correspondence with Arnauld* (Open Court Edn.), p. 74.

'This is what seems to me very hard to understand, that a body which has no motion can give itself motion. And if this is admitted, one of the proofs for the being of God is destroyed; namely the necessity for a first mover.'[19] Catholic orthodoxy saw its own powers as the culmination of a causal sequence which was traceable right back to God himself. It lived in a world where inert matter waited for the transmission of that energy whose only source was God, and it was happily satisfied that in matters which were spiritually crucial the line of transmission ran through the Church alone. But the very basis of Leibniz' thought is to be found in his new conception of substance as a non-material entity, a single and entirely individual being which carries in itself the pattern and the motive power of all its subsequent actions and passions (or passivities). The monad is itself a fulguration of the divine, and stands always in a primary relationship to the Monarch of spirits himself. There are implications here which might dismiss the pretensions of human authority. To the religious authoritarian the principle of mediation would seem to be essential. When a train begins to move the motion of the engine is first communicated to the adjacent truck and then to the remaining trucks in strict succession until the guard's van is reached. This communication of motion, or of force, is a kind of apostolic succession upon which the guard's van is entirely dependent for its motive power. Leibniz wished to remove this picture of the world and to replace it by a world where trains and successions are apparent rather than real, and where each individual substance is related directly to every other and reflects the changes which take place in all of them, including those which happen in the Monad of Monads himself. Consequently, the principle of mediation is left with only phenomenal value, for mediation is supplanted by the idea of concomitance (*convenance*), and Leibniz' metaphor of the choir replaces the Aristotelian picture of communicated impulses and a prime mover. It will be seen that, in terms of the kind of authority we have been discussing, Leibniz was envisaging a Protestant rather than a Catholic choir. If Leibniz is to be believed, every part of the universe has the whole written into it. The universe is self-authenticating, and it is not only Cartesian clear and distinct perception, the awareness of necessary truth, which is the authoritative ground of our

[19] Letter to Leibniz (Open Court Edn.), p. 204.

knowledge. Our knowledge of contingent facts, while variable and relatively less clear, is not different in kind but only in degree. Our normal view of the universe, when we are not confused or otherwise in a bad relational state, is a true perception of things as they really are, and this is guaranteed to us, not by the moral nature of God, as Descartes argued, but by the nature of substance itself; for the individual substance mirrors the universe, more or less clearly according to its own development, and in the soul monad this development is relatively high, so that it can be said that even its relationship with God is founded on identity rather than difference, or that the difference between the soul and God himself is one of degree rather than of kind.[20]

Like Descartes, Leibniz had a streak of orthodoxy in his make-up, but it did not fit into his philosophical scheme. He did not concede the existence, in any of the disciplines, of valid but esoteric knowledge for which the philosophical inquirer must acknowledge himself in debt to the adept. Instead, he was convinced of the possibility of relating all knowledge by means of a common logical instrument or calculus, so that when controversies arose either in a particular field of knowledge or between different fields, the apparent contradictions could be shown to be errors of calculation. In this, as in every phase of his thinking, Leibniz revealed the almost unlimited optimism for which he was duly lampooned by Voltaire. But it was not the purely religious optimism which Voltaire took it to be—a blind faith in the perfection of God who must, because of his perfection, order all things in the best possible way. It was a metaphysical optimism, grounded in his demonstration of the nature of the individual substance and of the collocation of substances which formed the world; and grounded not less on his conviction, based on the same metaphysical premises, that the potentiality of human reason was obstructed by no boundary of possibility and inhibited by no necessary limitations from a fullness of knowledge only second to that of God himself.

* * *

It is possible, at this stage, to discern a point of culmination in the movement of philosophical confidence which brought a neo-Hellenic sense of freedom and adventure to the eighteenth century.

---

[20] Letter to Arnauld, 6th October 1687 (Open Court Edn.), p. 231.

In both the rational and empirical camps there was a feeling of progress achieved and of immense possibilities of advance opening up. His theoretical difference of approach made little difference to the practical attitude of Leibniz, who was as keenly interested in the methods of experiment and observation as any of the English empiricists. Locke, on the other hand, may have had a much more restricted view of the nature of human intellectual processes, but he believed that Providence supplied all that we need for our purposes. On both sides there was a sufficient detachment to free speculation from the claims of authority. On the empirical side this is obvious, and the logic of Descartes' position pointed the same way. But even Leibniz' deference to the views of others and his respect for the past, not to mention his natural diffidence, must not lead us to suppose that he was less resolute about philosophical and scientific freedom. It was simply that his metaphysic made it impossible for him to ignore the significance of all that contributed to the present. But the authority of the past and of existing systems was not a confinement of souls; it was simply part of each individual nature, for predication belongs to the subject and not the subject to the predicate.

The nature of the case at this juncture may be expressed by saying that there appeared to be no essential information about man and his environment which was in principle beyond the reach of his power to investigate. The field was being cleared, so it seemed, for a sturdy and optimistic empiricism which was exactly suited to the approaching age of science. It is true that Locke's account of mind was a little bleak, but it suggested reliability. It seemed to describe psychological data in the simplest possible way and it placed the mind in a fairly direct and dependable relationship with the world of facts which was to be observed. Only let this confident affirmation of facts be joined to the new genius for calculation and no problems would be beyond the possibility of solution. So it must have seemed to the intelligent onlooker before the quiet voice of Hume carried the arguments of Locke a little further and pursued with greater rigour the logic of empiricism.

The result of Hume's work was an apparent undermining of the theoretical foundations not only of empiricism, but of all human knowledge. Locke had denied us any prior and private knowledge of the world and asserted our total reliance upon ideas which arose in the mind and which were simply copies or resemblances of qualities in the world outside. Berkeley, in his turn, raised doubts about the presumed reference of ideas to external and material reality by pointing out how difficult it is to bridge the gap between events in the mind and their supposed extramental causes. It remained for Hume to cast doubts upon the selfhood of the supposed self which received and compared such ideas and to throw doubt upon the trustworthiness and rationality of the idea-comparison process itself. 'The authority of the facts' has been mentioned as a possible refuge from the subjective confusion of dogmatic rationalism, but the conclusions of Hume seemed to be fatal alike to all pretensions of rational knowledge, whether deduced from so-called innate ideas or induced from experience. He cut away the slender tendrils which bound the Berkleian soul to its kindred and left our bundle of impressions in complete isolation; 'Let us chase our imagination to the heavens, or to the utmost limits of the universe; we never really advance a step beyond ourselves, nor can conceive any kind of existence, but those perceptions, which have appeared in that narrow compass. This is the universe of the imagination, nor have we any idea but what is there produced.'[21]

Having indicated our isolation and our unavoidable uncertainty about the relationship of impressions to their presumptive sources in a world of whose independent existence we can have no guarantee, Hume proceeded to cast doubt upon the processes by which we compare and relate those impressions, and the residual ideas which echo them, in order to reach new conclusions. It turned out that the connexions between our impressions or ideas are themselves exceedingly tenuous. It is difficult to see how we can reason from one idea to another. 'There is nothing, in any object, considered by itself, which can afford us a reason for drawing a conclusion beyond it; and, that even after the observation of the frequent or constant conjunction of objects, we have no reason to draw any inference concerning any object beyond those of which we have experience' (ibid., I.139). This estimate, if it is true, is fatal to rationalism and empiricism alike; for the mind, as Hume sees it, contains neither the innate capacities or intuitions which are assumed by the rationalist, nor the clear and relatable images of nature which empiricism requires.

[21] *Treatise* (Everyman Edn.), I.72.

Yet we have convictions of truth; stubborn beliefs about ourselves and the nature of our world. Where do these come from? and what degree of dependability should we attribute to them? In practice, says Hume, they suffice. He disclaims the title of sceptic and only demonstrates the sceptical conclusions to which his arguments seem to point because he wishes to show that the basis of our reasoning is custom. That does not invalidate it as a practical process, but we ought to be aware that our beliefs are more a matter of feeling than of cogitation. Hume incorporated the Cartesian criterion—the clearness and distinctness with which ideas are perceived—but he saw that our estimation of the degree of clearness and distinctness is not a matter for which we can provide any reliable calculus. We must be content with a sensitive estimate; yet if we are so content we make feeling the judge of truth rather than ratiocination. Hume accepts the limitations which are implied by this conclusion: 'It is not solely in poetry and music we must follow our taste and sentiment, but likewise in philosophy. When I am convinced of any principle, it is only an idea which strikes more strongly upon me. When I give the preference to one set of arguments against another, I do nothing but decide from my feeling concerning the superiority of their influence.'[22] He concludes that belief makes ideas imitate the effects of impressions (ibid., p. 120), but it is quite clear that some reason must be found to account for the inclination which we have to elevate certain ideas to a more vivid status. Presumably our feelings, which are the instruments of this process, are themselves moved by the quality of the original ideas. Hume allows for this in his theory of the association of ideas, according to which ideas which have a certain degree of affinity are mutually evocative; he also notices the additional force which is acquired by ideas to which we have become accustomed, or even addicted, by previous acceptance and constant repetition. In these circumstances ideas 'take such deep root, that it is impossible for us, by all the powers of reason and experience, to eradicate them' (ibid., p. 117). At this point Hume would surely have found it difficult to avoid the word 'conditioning' if it had been available with its modern connotation. 'I am persuaded that, upon examination, we shall find more than one half of those opinions that prevail among mankind be owing to education, and that the principles which are thus

[22] *Treatise*, I.105.

implicitly embraced, overbalance those which are owing either to abstract reasoning or experience' (ibid.).

All this constituted a very formidable challenge to the intellectual optimism of the time and in due course the challenge was met, more or less adequately and from differing points of view, by Kant and his assorted progeny in Germany, by the 'commonsense' philosophers, and by a new and somewhat perilous irrationalism which followed the Humian impasse as the magical cults and esoteric doctrines of the Hellenistic age followed the era of the Greek sceptics. As Lord Russell has written, 'The growth of unreason throughout the nineteenth century and what has passed of the twentieth is a natural sequel to Hume's destruction of empiricism.'[23] Up to the time of Hume, the two clear contestants for supremacy as the directors of human thought and action would seem to have been authority and reason. If there was a third way, it was not clearly seen. During a long and not very fruitful period the method of authority had been adopted, not only in matters of religion and morality, but in the field of science too. When Scheiner, the Jesuit, observed sunspots independently of Galileo, he was told quite firmly by his father-superior that the spots must be on his eyes or on his glasses: they could not be on the sun, for Aristotle made no mention of them. Sooner or later men were bound to see through this sort of nonsense, and we have been able to notice how this took place, and how the Renaissance, the Reformation, and the Enlightenment prepared the way for the development of that freedom of the mind which is not only a prerequisite of scientific progress, but which we should also regard as the necessary basis for the healthy development of political, ethical and religious ideas. But we have also come to the point where, if Russell is right, freedom itself becomes destructive of freedom and the very exercise of reason discovers evidence for the distrust of reason.

The sequel which might be expected is a recourse to irrationalism of one kind or another in the hope of finding new authority to replace those intellectual guarantees that have been discarded. Or there may be a simpler explanation. The vanguard of thought is the territory of a few men in any age and their leadership, however vivid and crucial its impact upon the thought of their time, is inevitably challenged and retarded by the counteraction of what

[23] *History of Western Philosophy*, p. 699.

Hegel might have thought a true Hegelian antithesis, the opposing force of prejudice and custom and sheer human inertia. Moreover, the old authorities persist. Diminished in stature and reduced in their following, they still retain a hold upon the imagination of a great many people who are not able, in any case, to discern what is happening in an age of progress and freedom, and who will persistently judge affairs by the index of material benefits. Perhaps both these factors were at work during the century which followed Kant's effort to rehabilitate empiricism and to unite it with rationalism in his own brand of idealism. Even if this be so, it is still not possible to judge which played the greater part, the tug of reaction or the sceptical challenge of Hume. To decide that, we should have to decide whether it is more true to say that philosophy is the child of history than to say that history is the child of philosophy.

We shall have to be content to indicate an observed tendency of thought without pretending to understand all its causes; and that tendency is the partial, post-Kantian movement away from disillusioned reason toward systems based on feeling and will. In so far as Kant was a critical philosopher, he was trying to re-assess the manner and validity of our knowledge of the world. Leibniz had, in Kant's view, 'intellectualized appearances, just as Locke . . . sensualized the concepts of the understanding',[24] and it was the avowed intention of the critical philosophy to reconcile the truth of rationalism with the truth of empiricism. It was insisted that no sense can be made of the world by trying to consider sense material apart from those operations of the mind which supply the frame, if not the form, of the finished picture. The work of Kant had immense influence, but if it was partly successful in vindicating the cause of reason, there was also much in it which nourished the adversaries of reason. First, Kant removed at least a large part of reality to a Platonic intelligible world and then he assumed that this noumenal realm was discontinuous with the phenomenal world. This looks like a new form of the Cartesian dualism, and its basis must surely be dogmatic and rational. So we find ourselves left with a new rationalism which contrives to embrace empirical data into the rational scheme and postulates a new empirical realm in the noumenal world, where the empirical cannot be observed. This can no longer be regarded as a solution,

[24] *Critique of Pure Reason* (Watson's trans.), p. 221.

though it gave new life to a movement of idealism whose influence is by no means exhausted. But Kant also left a legacy to the disciples of unreason. He relegated the problems of morality and the spiritual life to the sphere of the will, and it was with problems in these fields that many of his successors occupied themselves, for these were matters which were to attract increasing attention and controversy in the nineteenth century. Side by side with this aspect of Kant we must set Rousseau's exaltation of feeling. Hume had suggested that feeling might be the true arbiter in what we imagined were intellectual decisions. Rousseau accepted this suggestion and exhibited his conclusions in a life in which pathological sensitiveness was prized as a cardinal virtue.

If, for a while, the new procedures of science had developed side by side with philosophy in the rational atmosphere of the eighteenth century, the latter part of the century was to separate the lines of development once more until English empiricism and French materialism conceded the centre of the stage to post-Kantian German idealism. It had seemed enough to the age of Newton that reason was an accredited and entirely adequate tool for the manipulation of our material environment. The scientist may have been content, in subsequent generations, to cling to this limited hypothesis, for it was all that he needed for his particular task. But the naïvely dualistic world that nineteenth-century science inherited was unsatisfactory to the followers of Kant, who refused to be content with the working parallelism of minds and things manipulated, and yet were not ready for the materialist's assimilation of the minds to the manipulated, but sought instead to incorporate the phenomenal world into mind itself. Johann Gottlieb Fichte is a representative enough figure to consider at this point. Fichte's idealism was based upon the fact of consciousness, which he conceived to be a positive activity and not simply the passive reception of sensations. He thought of the ego in terms of true activity and took this action, or realized thought, to be the destination and fulfilment of man. But action produces reaction and in the same way the ego, by its very existence, delineates or even invents the non-ego. 'Without an ego there is no non-ego, no Object, no world. A world *per se*, a world of "*dinge an sich*" is unthinkable'.[25] There is, however, in Fichte's view, an inhibitor of action. In fact, the non-ego itself must

[25] Lewes, *History of Philosophy*, II.561.

inhibit the ego even while it affords it limited expression, for the end of the ego is freedom to be itself. Consequently there exists in the ego a pressure to be free, which is will. Will, then, is the creative factor of the ego, and it in turn seems to be directed by a norm or standard which Fichte calls duty. Our feeling for this required aim of the will is 'conscience', and so it is true to say that when God made conscience he made the world.

It does not seem to be necessary, for our present purpose, to plod farther into the deepening morass of German idealism. But one tendency must be noticed. It is evident that the 'rationalism' of the eighteenth century had proved too arid for the philosophers, however satisfactory it may have been to the scientists. Hence we must not be surprised to see science move off to attend more and more to its own concerns and to elaborate its own methods, while philosophy, which in Descartes and Leibniz lay so close to the centre of scientific endeavour, diverges to fulfil new functions in the more highly coloured world of literature, religion, and human relationships. Already certain key words—will, ego, feeling, strife —have crept into the philosophical vocabulary, each loaded with new meaning. If we set ourselves in the period it becomes clear that speculation is to take a new humanistic turn in very much the same way that Greek thought did in the time of Socrates. Only, this time, science, having more adequate resources and tools, and more fruitful concepts, will be able to accomplish its own ends in a state of relative independence. Its almost complete objectivity will deliver it from the problems of increasing self-awareness which periodically beset philosophers. The hint conveyed by Compte's positivism indicates the sensible outlook for men of science—or so it might seem. Ultimate considerations, if there are such things, are beyond our powers of investigation. This being so, far from lamenting our necessary ignorance, we must rejoice in a new freedom which follows the recognition of our limitations, and then apply ourselves with augmented vigour to the laws of phenomena.

Perhaps we may summarize, at this point, the elements in the work of the philosophers whom we have discussed in this chapter, which appear to have the most direct bearing upon the problem of authority in religion. Bacon was primarily concerned to achieve freedom of inquiry for his proposed science. He sought to justify this by an appeal to the 'twofold truth' doctrine, whether sincerely or not it is difficult to say. He believed, or professed to believe, that ethics rested on an original command of God. He believed, moreover, that natural phenomena conceal God. Theology, on both these counts, cannot pursue an inductive method. It must depend on revealed truth. Nature brings no knowledge of God, only wonder about Him. In each discipline we must appeal to the facts. In science, these are given by nature; in theology, they are given by revelation.

Hobbes found his own solution in assimilating the power of the Church to the power of the State. Even scripture is thought of by him as received from the hand of the sovereign. This, however, merely removes the problem to a new field. Instead of seeking to establish and certify the claims of religion, we have to establish those of the State, which then offers us a guaranteed religion.

Descartes presented a third possibility, implicit in his conclusion that the evaluation of truth is a function of the clarity of individual perceptions. The consequences of this for religion were very far-reaching. Descartes did not, of course, initiate religious subjectivism, but he initiated a movement of thought which sought to invest 'the authority of the subjective' with intellectual respectability.

Leibniz' attitude to religious authority would appear to have been influenced by his notion of continuity. He would have suspected his own thought if he had believed it to be utterly at variance with the formulations which enshrined the accumulated experience and wisdom of the Church: especially so because his own philosophy was deeply concerned with the subject matter of religious doctrine, and his 'world view' was in fact a theodicy. One gathers that his variance from the theological statements of the Church would not have distressed him (apart from considerations of a social nature—he was sensitive about the disapprobation of others) so long as he could regard his innovations as developments and not as discontinuities.

Leibniz also reinforced the Cartesian appeal to subjective experience. The monad exists for him in an unmediated relationship with God. The relationship must be unmediated, because communication is only an appearance and the reality behind it is the unfolding of the self. If his scheme of relationship is accepted, it is difficult to see a reason why one unit or aggregation of units should possess authority except on the ground that it happens to have a clearer perception, that it reflects the nature of the totality of things more accurately than most. But the justification for such a claim could only reside in what was perceived, and this is not the method of authority.

Little mention has been made of the effect of Locke's thought upon the problem of religious authority, perhaps because our interest was caught at a critical moment by the development which is associated with Hume, whereby empiricism reached an apparent impasse and a reaction took place in favour of theories which revalued the contribution to knowledge of the self, whether as intellect, will, or feeling. It may be mentioned in passing that Locke's direct contribution to the discussion of religious authority was of considerable importance. It has not been mentioned here because the intention has been to notice some of the chief movements of philosophical thought in the period which seem to have influenced theological opinion on the subject of authority. Locke's chief contribution to the subject was less by way of the philosophical doctrine most commonly associated with his name, than by the direct expression of his sociological and theological ideas. It is by reason of the latter that his name is so closely associated with the struggle for religious freedom and toleration—almost, one might say, in spite of his philosophy, for he writes as though he believed that in matters of religion knowledge is subservient to right feeling and Christ-like conduct—'Obedience to what is already revealed is the surest way to more knowledge'; 'the indispensable duty of all Christians' is 'to maintain love and charity in the diversity of contrary opinions, since Christianity is not a notional science but a rule of righteousness'.[26] On the face of it, this opinion does not agree with 'Reason must be our last judge and guide us in everything',[27] but there was no conflict so far as Locke himself could see. He believed that for the most part knowledge comes to us either from sensation or reflection, but that there are other communications of an extraordinary nature which come to us through the agency of other persons to whom we may be willing to credit a revelation from God.[28] The credibility of such alleged revelation must, however, be examined by reason, which thereby remains the final criterion in religion.

[26] Quoted from R. H. Bainton's *The Travail of Religious Liberty* (Lutterworth Press, 1953).
[27] *Essay on Human Understanding*, IV.19.14.   [28] *Essay*, IV.18.2.

Hume's sceptical conclusions were followed, as we have seen, by a cheerful acceptance of what are usually thought to be the facts of experience and of the need to fall back on feeling when reason fails to provide us with the guidance we need. We have seen that some philosophers took this hint and began to re-examine the part played by will and feeling, so that in the nineteenth century a new wave of subjectivism grew up alongside the still self-conscious objectivism of science. As we come now to consider the ways in which theologians have thought about the problem of authority, we shall see that the thought of philosophers and theologians has beeen closely related. As a preliminary judgement it may be enough to say that theology has shown itself, in this matter of authority at least, to be extremely sensitive to the tendencies of philosophical opinion. The need to justify this view will be kept in mind as we turn to the mainly expository tasks of the next chapter.

CHAPTER FIVE

MODERN THEOLOGY AND THE PROBLEM OF AUTHORITY

'**M**ODERN' is a rather nebulous qualification in this connexion, since it is sometimes used to indicate the post-Reformation period in theology, more commonly the theology of the last hundred years or so, and sometimes the theology of the present day. In the present chapter the second field of reference will be what we have chiefly in mind. First, however, it is necessary to preface what has to be said about the modern period by a short account of the sources which generated the more recent discussion of authority in religion. Three sources only need to be distinguished at this point. The first is the Catholic tradition embodied more particularly in the Roman Catholic Church; the second is the theology of the reformers and its subsequent development, especially in this country; the third is the profound influence of the work of the philosophers of the post-Reformation period, of whom some of the more representative have been mentioned in the previous chapter.

We shall not embark on a separate discussion of the validity of the concept of authority in the pre-Reformation Church. It is sufficient to say that the central issue of the Reformation was the problem of authority, and that the authority which the Reformers challenged was the authority of the Pope. The Papacy had long been established as the supreme authority in matters of doctrine and matters of discipline within the Church and it had for some time enjoyed very considerable authority over the affairs of the nations of Europe. By the time of the Reformation much of the Pope's secular authority had been pared away, but his claim to spiritual authority had not been effectively challenged. Whatever else one may think of the old system of authority, it was delightfully simple. The Pope was the viceroy of God and governed the Church in his name and by his authority. It was assumed that when the Pope spoke the Church spoke, and he spoke with an authority equal to that of the Bible and as the sole interpreter of the Bible's meaning—this was the position with regard to spiritual authority laid down by the Council of Trent, convened shortly before Luther's death. This authority was not thought of as transmitted, as in the case of a bishop. As soon as the decision of the cardinals about a new Pope was known to themselves, they venerated the man whom God had chosen and to whom authority was thereby given. It is significant that the subsequent ceremony of coronation had nothing to do with the conferment of authority but was rather a celebration and recognition of the fact of papal authority.

The Pope still enjoys this plenitude of power and the Roman Curia is only the instrument of his government. The College of Cardinals, the chief and highest of his agencies of government, was apparently at one time in danger of establishing an oligarchy, the cardinals being few and very powerful in the fifteenth and sixteenth centuries. Against this tendency the Popes successfully asserted themselves as absolute rulers by increasing the number of the cardinals and curbing the powerful position of the consistory.[1]

Suffice it to say that the whole Christian Church was not altogether satisfied with either the theory or the consequences of the notion of an absolute religious authority vested in any man or body of men. Before we look at the modern discussion of the subject, we should perhaps look briefly at the major alternative theories of authority that were developed by the Reformers. I am indebted to Rupert Davies[2] for the substance of what follows.

Luther sought objective authority in the Bible—'All that the Pope ordains, does, and carries out, I will see to it that I test it previously by the Holy Scriptures' (ibid., p. 25). The Scriptures were for him the Word of God, though he thought less highly of some parts than others, in so far as some parts set forth less clearly the Gospel of Christ (which for Luther was very closely bound up with the doctrine of Justification by Faith). His test was, '*Treibt es Christum oder nicht?*' (ibid., p. 33). The word of God was recognizably such by its correspondence, not simply with this doctrine, but with the Christian experience of justification, or sense of having been forgiven. There is a strong subjective element here, but Luther still claimed that the Word of God was an external,

---

[1] See Heinrich Scharp, *How the Catholic Church is Governed* (Herder-Nelson), English trans., 1960, p. 23.
[2] *The Problem of Authority in the Continental Reformers* (Epworth Press, London, 1946).

infallible authority. He recognized a peculiar degree of authority in the Church, which still had the power to distinguish the Word of God from the words of men; but by 'the Church' he presumably meant the true Church, as he understood it, the whole body of true believers. The Church, however, cannot reverse what has been decided by the Word of God. In the words of Davies, 'Luther set up the totalitarian, omnicompetent Word of God in place of the totalitarian omnicompetent Church of the Middle Ages' (ibid., p. 54).

Luther's concept of the authority in religion is criticized for its concealed subjectiveness—the Word of God was for him subjectively discerned—and for its static conception of revelation. The Word is set forth once and for all. Davies concludes that in any case we have found no such word of God, infallible, final, and purely external (for Luther conceived it as external, and did not himself seem aware of the strong subjective factor he had introduced).

Zwingli, a more intellectual and less emotional man than Luther, felt that the question to be decided was, 'What is the absolutely trustworthy source of truth, philosophical speculation embodied in the decrees of the Roman Church, or the Bible?' (ibid., p. 68). In his view, the Bible was self-authenticating and quite independent of the guarantees of the Church or of individual experience. He appealed to the method of the Fathers when they refuted the heretic Arius, 'the scripture expounds the scripture'. What authority the true Church possesses (the company of all true believers and not the domain of the Pope) is derived from its obedience to the Word of God.

In Zwingli there is less stress on the normative value of the feelings of the individual, though the element of personal experience is not completely absent. The possession of a pious heart is still needed to discern the Word of God (see ibid., p. 87). Davies points out the difficulty of attributing absolute authority to scripture when that scripture is a body of literature which gives expression to the corporate experience of the Church over a period of time. This corporate experience may be what we should mean by 'church' in this connexion and, if it was the deciding factor, absolute authority can hardly belong to the scripture apart from the Church. The section on Zwingli concludes with a reference to Zwingli's suggestion that the Bible itself is an object of faith, and that it is this faith which reveals the authority.

For Calvin, too, religious authority was wholly bound up with the Word of God. That was the source of truth. God did declare Himself in creation, but we failed to recognize Him, so He revealed himself in his Word. Calvin uses *verbum dei* indifferently with the term 'scriptures', and by that he indicates the Bible as we have it now, though without the Apocrypha. Both Testaments have the same authority, though the judicial and ceremonial laws of the Old Testament do not apply to us who are not Jews. The Apostles were the 'certain and authentic secretaries of the Holy Spirit' (ibid., p. 114).

Calvin, however, believed just as fervently in the authority of the Church as the community of the elect, and believed too that Christ has 'appointed pastors and teachers, by whose lips he might edify the people; He has invested them with authority' (ibid., p. 121), but this authority is not for men, but for the task of ministry, and the ministry is authenticated by the Word of God which it must embody and reveal. The Word of God generates the Church and all its essential rule. Regulations may be added which have no direct warrant in scripture, but they are not to be regarded as binding upon all Christians. His criticism of the Roman rites was not so much that they were without scriptural warrant as that they were obligatory. On the other hand, Calvin suspected subjectivism and condemned pretenders to private revelation who were not subject to 'The Word of God'.

How does Calvin consider the Bible to be attested as the Word of God? Apparently we are able to sense the fact directly, as we can distinguish sweet from bitter. 'The Scripture offers, unasked, a sense of its truth' (ibid., p. 139). Reason attests the Bible's message, but proofs are not themselves enough to awaken faith, it is the testimony of the Holy Spirit that convinces us that a book comes from God.

According to Davies, Calvin is free from Luther's subjective defect, though like Zwingli, he is open to the charge that to assert the authority of the Bible is to assert the authority of the Church which produced and authorized it. Neither Calvin nor Zwingli faced the problem of the need for an infallible interpreter if the infallible message of the Bible is to be communicated to men of ordinary understanding who do not know what this difficult and by no means univocal book is saying to us. Davies, however, is impressed by the suggestive value of Calvin's 'internal element' in

THEOLOGY AND AUTHORITY

authority: 'If we say that the source of authority in general is the coerciveness of truth and the inner testimony of the Holy Spirit working together, we have a view which is worthy of very serious consideration' (ibid., p. 149).

In his conclusion, Davies asks why the Reformers were unable to solve the problem which confronted them. He believes that it was because they were unable to free themselves from the medieval error that the source of authority must be entirely outside the individual. Perhaps we shall be in a better position to judge whether that was in fact an error when we have had something to say about the relationship between religious authority and the religious experience of the individual.

From this phase of Protestant thought a double legacy was handed down. Luther's contribution to this was the concept of an objective Word of God, if only we can find it, while Calvin's main contribution centres round the assertion that 'true knowledge comes from the interaction of the knower, the known, and the Spirit of God' (ibid., p. 154). In addition to this, we need to remember the strong subjective element in Luther's criteria for perceiving what is the Word of God. Zwingli shared Luther's objectivity about scripture and added, 'the scripture expounds the scripture', in an effort to skirt round a possible subjective reliance on any kind of human judgement. It is fairly clear, then, that the Protestant substitute for the authoritative Church of the middle ages is to be found either in an objective 'Word of God', or a subjective experience, or some blend of the two.

While we are considering the sources of the Protestant attitude to authority, we may perhaps include the philosophical influences which were discussed in the last chapter. In pre-Reformation society philosophy and theology had been so closely related as to be almost a single discipline, and it is to be expected that their mutual influence would be considerable, even after the separation to which Bacon looked forward. We need not concern ourselves with the influence which theology exerted on philosophy, but we can hardly fail to notice how sensitive theology was to the work of philosophers, particularly to the work that was done during the period of philosophical development from Descartes to Hegel: or it may be the case that a common spirit informed both theologians and philosophers. It would obviously be reckless, for instance, to trace subjectivism in Protestantism to the introspective method of

Descartes. For the modern period it must be traced to the theology of the Reformers. Yet the appeal to 'inward experience' cannot have been unaffected by the emergence of a philosophical background which must have seemed to lend support to its convictions about the true ground of knowledge. The Protestant appeal to individual experience was, as we have seen, a by-product of Luther's attempt to find objective authority in the Bible. It proved difficult to separate the objective record from its subjective apprehension, especially if the reader happened to be vividly conscious of a new phase in his own awareness of relationship with God, as Luther was, and therefore not in a particularly objective frame of mind. Luther's thought was dominated by one doctrine, the doctrine which declares the forgiving attitude of God to a man who has faith in Christ. In this sacred interchange, Luther experienced a tremendous sense of personal release, and it is not surprising that henceforward this deep personal feeling was to become a touchstone by which was judged the genuineness of religious profession throughout much of Protestantism.

The religious side of this appeal to personal experience can be seen in the Puritan doctrine of an 'inner light', in the Pietist movement on the Continent, and the 'enthusiasts' in England, with their exaggerated claim of personal inspiration which proved so disturbing to the staid orthodoxy of the eighteenth century. Theological substance and balance was given to this subjective tendency by the writings of William Law, *inter alia*, and by his insistence that 'Christ is in every man'. Wesley (at the time confused with the 'enthusiasts') followed with an undoubted appeal to the authority of experience, but an experience subject to the pragmatic test of character and action. He had little time for so-called religious experience if it did not make better citizens of those who laid claim to it. From that point the line of succession runs down through the Evangelicals, the products of the Methodist movement who remained within the Church of England, through Coleridge and F. D. Maurice and the religious backwash of the Romantic movement. On the Continent this 'theology of experience' culminated in Schleiermacher, who grounded dogma 'in the religious consciousness, and said, in so many words, again and again, that dogma is simply the statement, in the form of logical propositions, of the states of feeling which are characteristic of Christian piety'.[3]

[3] Henry Bett, *Studies in Religion* (Epworth Press, 1929), p. 18.

THEOLOGY AND AUTHORITY

It is not difficult to see how easily the philosophical appeal to inner experience from Descartes onwards would interweave with this aspect of theological development, though one would be very hesitant to indicate just how the influence operated without an extended historical study. In the case of Wesley, who might with fairness be regarded as a chief representative of this theological emphasis in the formative period, we do at least know that his interest in philosophy lasted long after the Oxford period and that he was well-acquainted with the works of Berkeley, Locke and Hume. He was critical of the immaterialism of Berkeley,[4] and he had no good word to say about Hume's scepticism;[5] but he admired Locke. It is true that in the ecclesiastical orthodoxy of the period of his tutorship at Oxford he sounded dubious about the enthusiasm of his charges for Locke's essay on authority (*Letters*, I.136), and twenty years later he was still a little suspicious of the *Essay on Human Understanding* (*Journal*, 6th December 1756), but in later years he came to have the highest regard for Locke's work and went so far as to include the *Essay* in a short list of recommendations for the library of a small school for girls (he had been asked by the headmistress, a Miss Bishop of Keynsham, for a list of books to improve young persons from twelve to twenty!). Wesley quoted with approval the basic postulate of Locke's epistemology, '*Nihil est in intellectu quod non prius in sensu*'.[6] Extracts from the *Essay* were published from time to time in the *Arminian Magazine* (forerunner of the *Methodist Magazine*). It may also be relevant to mention a letter which Wesley wrote to Joseph Benson in 1768. Benson was teaching classics at Wesley's school at Kingswood as a preparation for Oxford and ordination. The letter begins: 'Dear Joseph, You have now twenty more volumes of the *Philosophical Translations* [Wesley's own translations and abridgements of the works of the great philosophers, designed chiefly to broaden the reading of his preachers], Malebranche [included in the list of studies for the fourth year] and some other books are coming. Logic you cannot crack without a tutor: I must read it to Peter and you if we live to meet.' He closes with a touch that is characteristic: 'But beware you be not swallowed up in books; an ounce of love is worth a pound of learning.'[7]

---

[4] *Letters* (Standard Edn.), I.23ff.   [5] See *Journal*, V.458.
[6] See Macdonald, *Ideas of Revelation* (Macmillan, 1959), p. 251.
[7] *Letters*, V.110 and note.

This little digression is not intended to show that Wesley's theology of experience was generated by the line of introspective philosophy which we trace from Descartes, the development of which exerted such a profound influence on the thought of Wesley's contemporaries. But it does indicate, what we believe a fuller study would make quite clear, that he sat close to the philosophical developments of his time, that he was fully alive to their bearing on his theological position, and that education and theology in his period were both deeply sensitive to the flux of philosophical ideas.

So far we have noticed only one of the contributory streams which have fed modern theological thinking on the subject of authority—the appeal to the experient subject, which originates, for the post-Reformation Church, in the theology of Luther. The second stream we have in mind owed much more to philosophy and much less to the theologians of the Reformation. It took the form of theological rationalism, and its theological roots go back beyond the Reformation to the rationalism of Johannes Scotus Erigena and those others of the medieval schoolmen who followed his lead. For the present purpose we need not look further back than the Cambridge Platonists of the seventeenth century. Their roots lay in Platonic or Neo-platonic ideas, but they were influenced by Descartes, with whom Thomas More corresponded. It is enough to say that they believed in the ability of a truly rational man to adumbrate a satisfactory theology by using his innate ideas, his powers of reasoning, and the given facts of the natural world.

We meet this kind of theological rationalism again, but pushed to further lengths, in the teaching of the Deists of the eighteenth century. In one sense Deism was a reaction from the subjective tendencies of 'enthusiasts' of all kinds who made seemingly impertinent claims about personal revelation. The times may not have been altogether gentlemanly, but the approved manner in religion was a cool and reasonable dubiety. There was more in Deism, however, than reaction to excess. It stood squarely in the rationalist tradition which had been revived in the philosophical renaissance and it bequeathed a theological legacy which is still by no means expended. Its primary characteristics seem to have been a belief in the sufficiency of unaided reason to discover, by its own operations, and by inspecting the data presented in nature, all that we need to know about God and, secondly, a deep suspicion of any kind of supposed revelation or miracle—of anything, in fact, which might discourage the notion that God was other than an absentee landlord who constructed the universe and then withdrew, taking no part in its activity. He is discoverable, in principle, through his creative achievement, but impassive and remote.

Before we explore the destination of this stream any farther, we might notice the criticism of Deism offered by H. D. Macdonald (*Ideas of Revelation*, pp. 51ff). Macdonald complains that if each man is to follow his own untrammelled reason, then 'There is no objective standard, for the criterion of truth lies in the knowing subject, not in the object to be known'. This, Macdonald says, is like the monadism of Leibniz and overlooks the social nature of the self. The reference, one feels, is not a happy one, for in the system of Leibniz monads were only solitary in their selfhood. No one has been more insistent than Leibniz upon the need to recognize the orientation of the self in society. The monad, after all, reflected, though imperfectly and from its own point of view, every other monad in the universe. The end to which Leibniz pointed, and which he saw to be already partly realized (or it could not, from his point of view, be the end), was a divine society and not a state of individual perfection. Individual perfection was, for him, a perfect integration into the family of spirits.

Leaving aside the reference to Leibniz, the form of Macdonald's criticism is of interest, if it is not novel, and we shall have to consider in due course whether it is true that a state of mind can be said to be a criterion of truth. Macdonald's second criticism is that Deist doctrine can never say any more than nature has said. If this is true, it must also be true that science can never say any more than nature has said. That is arguable, but only if one broadens nature to include the scientist. The criticism can only imply an undesirable restriction of the knowledge which is so to be gained if it assumes that nature is restricted to some 'material' and extra-human sphere. The Deists did in fact regard nature in this rather limited way, but they need not have done. The criticism would have to be re-examined if we found it possible to define nature in a much wider sense, as Dr Raven suggested in his Gifford Lectures;[8] a sense which would include saints as well as filterable viruses. If it really was their defective view of nature

---

[8] *Natural Religion and Christian Theology* (Cambridge, 1953), I.3.

which presented the Deists with an impossible initial handicap, they should surely be criticized on that ground before their reliance on reason and nature is condemned altogether. We would feel ourselves that any criticism which assumes a dichotomy which puts human nature, with all its associated phenomena, in one category, and the rest of nature in another, rests on a decidedly contrived and artificial basis. Everything else we know about man and the civilization he has created identifies him as part of the natural world.

The challenge of Deism was met and overcome, but the rationalistic tendency which produced it persisted, though the theological manifestations which it produced were often remote from Deism. In some cases there was an attempted return to 'pure' reason in the tradition of Platonic idealism, and in the other cases there was always an optimistic belief in the competence of reason to make sense of the facts. It is in the latter sense that the empirical and critical methods of the nineteenth century theological liberals have a generic affinity with the earlier rationalism. The Deists had shared the same optimism of the ability of reason to discover all that man needs to know of himself, his world, and God, if it is presented with the facts—only the facts, for the liberals, included the data in which revelation was alleged to be embedded as well as the data of the natural world more narrowly defined. It is generally supposed that the liberal movement began in Germany, where the relationship between theology and philosophy had remained more intimate; to spread from there, in due course, to this country. There were, however, two related but distinguishable aspects of liberalism. One was chiefly concerned with the application of the methods of literary and historical criticism to the Bible (this was chiefly German in origin), and the other was largely occupied with the liberation of religion from the apparent confinements of traditional dogma and was concerned to promote a *rapprochement* with the rapidly unfolding discoveries of science. It was understandably unbearable for anyone who belonged by affinity to the intellectual or rational tradition in theology to feel that their loyalty to the fixed points of dogma, in so far as it was apparently irreconcilable with an acceptance of the discoveries of science, was pulling them away from the side of the intellectuals whose spirit and interests they shared and leaving them in the more sombre company of those who preferred 'a resolute ignorance'.[9] (The phrase is Coleridge's.) A navigator finds his way with the aid of a fixed North Pole and a free compass. The theological unrest of the nineteenth century started from the uncomfortable feeling that the Church was navigating to a predetermined North with the dubious aid of a compass which had been nailed in the desired position by somebody's father. The free compass was reason, and the Liberals were determined to steer whatever course it might indicate.

The liberal theologians and biblical critics were not the only proponents of reason in the theological field. There was a considerable movement of Idealism which looked to Kant and Hegel for its inspiration and sought to combat the prevailing agnosticism by restoring the metaphysical basis of theology by philosophical means. In an age of science the old miraculous assurances of God's reality and power were no longer looked upon as suitable data for the basis of a religious metaphysic, but Kant had indicated that the data of the physical world had no real significance apart from the creative and systematizing activity of mind, and Hegel had provided the fruitful hypothesis of a God who reveals himself through the process of development, and who stands at the end of any investigation (into anything) which is pushed far enough, as the Ultimately True, the Unavoidable All, the Absolute. Philosophical Idealism was still intellectually respectable, so it provided a hopeful speculative framework for theologians or theistically inclined philosophers who could not so far divorce themselves from the spirit of the age as to accept a ready-made theism on the authority of the Church or the Bible.

This was the general background of the renewed search for an understanding of the nature of authority in religion which has characterized the modern period. 'Modern', as we have already indicated, is a very indefinite adjective, so we will make it more precise, and will turn our attention now to some of the leading developments which have taken place since, in 1890, James Martineau published a study of the nature of religious authority which he called *The Seat of Authority in Religion*.[10] The main thesis of this work will be discussed later, but in the meantime here is a passage which will help to fill out our summary of the nineteenth-century theological scene: 'The faith of Christendom,

---

[9] Cf. L. E. Elliott Binns, *English Thought 1860-1900, The Theological Aspect*, p. 20.
[10] London, Longmans, Green.

essentially historical, has inherited its clearest memories from its primitive times, and turned towards them a look of regretful homage; but thrown into the contests of the passing hour, and coexisting since the Reformation with an unexampled progress of discovery, it could not remain purely retrospective, the passive trustee of departed sanctities. It was impelled to learn the language of a new time, and show its unexhausted fitness for the human soul, if it would vindicate its place in a universe so changed. This self-adaptation to the wants of a later culture created the whole religious literature, and much of the speculative philosophy, of modern Europe. Natural science, crowned with dazzling triumphs, affected every department of thought with admiration of her precise method and her favourite evidence of sense; and religion became fascinated, and undertook to shape herself into logical and objective form' (ibid., p. 172). Thus, says Martineau, Christianity 'receded from the high ground of religious authority, and descended into the field of intellectual conflict' (ibid., p. 172). Perhaps the most drastic step which had to be taken was the critical re-examination and re-assessment of religious literature as a whole, and of the Bible in particular. As we look back on the process it may be felt that even the most crucial part of the written tradition, the New Testament itself, did not emerge in very bad shape from the critical process to which it was submitted; or if our point of view is different, we may feel that grievous damage was done. On the whole, the verdict has been reasonably encouraging to Christian faith. But for Christians who had to carry their Christian faith and practice through the time of controversy, it must have been difficult to persuade themselves that their dubiety and uncertainty were produced by a process which might benefit the Christian religion in the long run. Their immediate concern was with the fact that they were being asked to stand for an undetermined time upon uncertain and shifting ground. Coming North by the Watling Street one may see a notice in one of the Midland mining districts: 'Warning, this road is liable to subsidence.' The traveller is not asked to take any action about the incipient peril. Nothing may happen to him, or he and his car may suddenly disappear into a hole in the ground. It was to be expected that the majority of Christians, when they found themselves in theoretical circumstances of a similar kind, would try to remove themselves from this uncertain territory as rapidly as

THEOLOGY AND AUTHORITY

possible, or would at least insist that the offending notices be covered over.

A reminder of Martineau's own criteria for assessing the acceptibility, for doctrinal purposes, of given New Testament passages, may serve to indicate some of the difficulties of the road which Christians were being asked to traverse. The following are the tests which Martineau applies to passages in the synoptic gospels which purport to give information about the life and teaching of Jesus: '(1) Whenever, during or before the ministry of Jesus, any person in the narrative is made to speak in language, or refer to events, which had their origin at a later date, the report is incredible as an anachronism. (2) Miraculous events cannot be regarded as adequately attested in the presence of natural causes accounting for belief in their occurrence. (3) Acts and words ascribed to Jesus which plainly transcend the moral level of the narrators authenticate themselves as His; while such as are out of character with His spirit, but conform with theirs, must be referred to inaccurate tradition' (ibid., p. 577).

This will serve as a fair sample of the attempts which were made to introduce 'rational' criteria—as distinct from the somewhat more careful rules of the historico-critical schools. It is obvious that Martineau's rules are anything but scientific. Errors of the anachronistic variety referred to in his first rule do not call for the excision of the offending passages, but for a patient investigation of the reason for their inclusion. We may indeed find ourselves dealing with intrusions of a later age, but that will itself open new fields of inquiry. If we investigate in the spirit of the first rule, we begin by ruling out of court precisely that feature of the teaching of Jesus which it is the business of a critical theology to investigate. There is no great question about the moral probity of Jesus, the questions have been about his super-historical insight.

Again, we are told that if a miraculous event is recorded, we may excuse ourselves the trouble of investigation if there are natural causes near at hand which might provide a rational explanation. But in fact we possess no such simple yardstick to measure the miraculous and to distinguish it from the nonmiraculous, and the tendency of the truly 'scientific' scholar would be to ask much simpler questions: not, 'Could this sort of thing happen?', but, 'When was this written and by whom?', 'What was the author trying to convey? What, in fact, is the strength of the evidence that some such occurrence took place or, at least, that someone had good reason to believe that it had taken place?' It is, of course, possible that the mud which Jesus put on the blind man's eyes possessed therapeutic qualities, or that a suggestive action was sufficient to disperse what may have been a functional condition, and if we resort to such explanations we will remove the problem of the miraculous element from the story. But the real point at issue is not the methodology of first-century medicine, but the reason why such stories were told about Jesus.

Martineau's third rule is a similar illustration of the lack of rule which sometimes served to provide outlets for the exuberance of the critical spirit. It is fairly clear, one would think, that acts and words ascribed to Jesus can only be crossed out of the record if their provenance is fatally suspect—because, in other words, there is good reason to believe that they formed no part of the original text. If we are to construct our own theoretical characterization of Jesus and then strike out all that does not appear to harmonize with it, then all pretence of rational procedure must be dropped. If the gospels ascribe words and acts to Jesus which are inconsistent with the general character of his recorded words and acts, then we may conclude, among other things, that the record is inaccurate (as Martineau did), or that Jesus sometimes acted out of character, or that this is a glimpse of his true character, or that the discrepancy is an indication that the ancient writer had more scruples than his modern critic. There are many other possible conclusions open to us, but we may not use scissors and paste to arrive at a neat and consistent characterization.

We simply record, however, that theological liberalism, bearing the legend of science and the historico-critical method upon its shield, sometimes struck blows of a wholly unscientific character in its desire to break down the ancient strongholds of superstition and sacrosanct tradition. Once the creation stories had been safely and understandably relegated to the realm of myth and legend, the way was open to dismiss, in the same way, any other material which did not fit neatly into a given critical reconstruction. The theological consequences of this procedure were remarkable. The theologian was freed from the obligation to take into account the whole teaching of the Bible and of Christian tradition. Instead, he could select such material as fitted his purpose and, having thereby arrived at a 'simple' and 'primitive' form of

Christianity, he could strike out all material hostile to his thesis on the ground that it was inconsistent with simple and primitive Christianity. This, one hopes, is not an altogether unfair way of describing Harnack's method in *What is Christianity?* (trans. of *Das Wesen des Christentums*, Berlin, 1900).

If we add the effects of this exuberant criticism of written tradition to those of the prolonged attack upon ecclesiastical tradition which we have already considered, we will not be surprised to find that in the early years of this century some Christian theologians were beginning to consider the question of authority with new earnestness. 'Man is . . . left without any firm footing on which to wage the unchanging conflict with the world, the devil, and the flesh. No authority either without or within seems to remain, with which he might face the many attractions which allure his senses and the many desires which corrupt his will. Yet the need for such an authority continues as of old.' So wrote John Oman in 1902,[11] and his was one of many voices which expressed the urgency of the search for a new concept of authority which would not only satisfy the desire for a new ground and source for religious belief and practice, but would also be agreeable to the new standard of critical perceptiveness which had spread from the scientific disciplines to the field of theological study.

We are now to consider three representative works of this period which together indicate the nature and direction of the search for authority. The first is the work of John Oman which is quoted above, and the title, *Vision and Authority*, indicates the intention of the book. Oman's chief concern is to reconcile authority and freedom and to dissuade those who argue that prudence requires us to accept an imperfect authority rather than suffer the consequences of having none. This narrows our search, and enables us to discard those would-be authorities whose relationship to truth is suspect . . . 'obscurantism is already unbelief' (ibid., p. 23). He argues that there is not a single source of authority, but the interaction of an internal and an external authority. No merely external authority can be compelling, and 'the highest creed taught merely from without becomes superstition' (ibid., p. 24). The real authority for religion will be found in the kind of vision of the infinite and eternal which certain fishermen of Galilee enjoyed, and which the childlike mind may

[11] *Vision and Authority* (London, Hodder and Stoughton), p. 20.

still attain. 'It is nothing else than a demand that man shall follow utterly the leading of his own spiritual insight, neither looking with the eyes of others, nor suffering hesitation and preconception to blind his own. It requires us not to be subject, but to be truly free.' To attain this kind of simple insight into the truth we need the help of others, but the authority of others is stagnation, for there is no Pope of vision. In spite of our philosophical quandaries about the problems of perception, we do not in practice doubt the trustworthiness of our eyesight to perform its appropriate functions. Spiritual insight, he argues, is capable of giving the same kind of synoptic view of the world, and its view has a like authority. Though the Church may offer infallible doctrine and scripture, and the ministrations of a priesthood which depends on the certainty of office, not the uncertainty of character, this does not excuse us if we surrender individual judgement and choice: 'We cannot submit to any representative of God on any less sure credentials than we should require to submit to God himself' (ibid., p. 73).

Yet this vision is not exercised in solitude, so that the revelation of God is a work of the race. History, therefore, has an important status in individual vision, and the progress of the individual is to some extent an education. To this extent we build on the foundation of the apostles and prophets, and must be true to our spiritual ancestry. This ancestry and kinship is the true Church, yet whatever authority is conceded to it must be acknowledged in freedom. The authority of scripture is of a similar order. It is not to be used to silence individual judgement or to close the eyes of insight. Jesus himself did not use the scriptures as a final warrant for belief; in this he was noticed to be quite unlike his contemporaries. The intercourse of writer and reader is an exchange of experience, not of command and obedience. Christ himself, the peak of the process of revelation, pursued this same method of exchanged experience. He did not merely transmit tradition, but offered his own unique insights, and 'He insisted on basing what he taught on the authority of their own hearts and consciences' (ibid., p. 110). 'Only by ecclesiastical juggling is he turned into a potentate who will tolerate no difference of doctrine and no variety of service' (ibid.) He commended Peter, not for learning his lesson accurately, but for his own insight into the truth about his Master, and the true succession of authoritiveness in the Church is a succession, not of office, but of insight and love. One might suppose that this kind of authority would be difficult to delineate, and would in any case be imprecise in its pronouncements. It is true that the theologian must now be content with something at once greater and less than the old mechanical certainties, 'But to receive anything on the assertion of another, though it be an infallible Church, is not knowledge' (ibid., p. 182). Authority which rests on freedom and individual vision realized and shared in the society of the Church, has at least the vitality of an organic process. If we are not satisfied with this, may it not be because 'we wish an authority which can dominate men without being required to win loyalty of their hearts, and which can maintain in them a careful regard to religious observances without being required to work in them personal faith and consecration' (ibid., p. 185).

For Oman, the true attitude of authority is summed up by the saying of Jesus: 'All ye are brethren, and one is your teacher.' There is no command to assent to a static truth, but the patience of the teacher until we learn and receive. 'The pursuit of truth is a high endeavour in which no fellow mortal can be more to us than our brother. To accept our brother's conclusions, without ourselves attempting to reach them, is not to honour either God or our brother by our meekness, but to dishonour both by our slackness' (ibid., p. 190). Oman expresses this in another way: 'Truth is not true except on personal conviction'. But this does not appear to be intended as an epistemological proposition so much as a psychological one. On the other hand, it may have been a foreshadowing of the kind of existential relativism which is said to be found in Paul Tillich. All this may sound like a return to the extreme individualism of the Puritan 'inner light', but Oman to some extent guarded against the extremes of subjectivism by distinguishing the worldly authority of the Church from a higher authority inherent in the visionary society which is the true Church. The former authority is that of custom and command, enhanced and fortified by a gradual accession of power and prestige which owe a lot to the work of successful ecclesiastical leaders and the impressiveness of the organization itself. Beyond and above that, however, is a community of vision which, by its very nature, acts as a touchstone to evaluate the vision of the individual.

The second work which must be considered in this connexion is

The Principle of Authority by P. T. Forsyth.[12] Like Oman, Forsyth expected to discover ultimate religious authority in the Christian experience—'Even Rome admits that in the last resort the *seat* of authority is in the soul' (ibid., p. 10). But what establishes the authoritativeness is more than the impression created on the mind; it is, in fact, the Christian revelation and the Cross. In this sense, an authority is not a limit, but a source of power, an augmentation (*auctoritas*). The religious authority for which he was searching could only be an act of God, external to us but fully personal and therefore communicable to us.

When we look for certainty in religion, we are not to look for a rock to stand on, a fixed and final foundation. We are to look for a fertile soil to sustain our growth; 'The reality in religion is not something to stand on, but something to live from' (ibid., p. 36). Christian certainty is a state of the soul which we call faith, not simply a truth held by it. He agreed that the seat of authority, seen in this light, was subjective. 'It is certain' means 'I am certain'. But that is not the source of authority. 'Nothing, truly, can be final authority which is not experienced, but it is not authoritative *because* it is experienced' (ibid., p. 50). 'The real ground of our certitude ... is the nature of the thing of which we are sure, rather than the nature of the experience in which we are sure' (ibid., p. 52). (He does not explain how the two may be disengaged.) Authority, in this sense, is a purely religious idea. When it appears in politics it is purely relative, and in science it has no place at all.

How, then, do we go beyond the subjective limitations of 'I am certain' to the clearer authority of 'It is certain'? We must apply ourselves afresh to the fundamental fact of Christianity, which is the fact of the identity, person and work of Jesus Christ. But even in the subjective element there is a givenness which makes what is virtually an external demand upon us. It does not appeal so much to our intelligence as to our will. 'There are imperatives which are independent of our subjective whim, but which make themselves felt with a spiritual necessity in the deep interior of our personal will. They embody a certain intelligence, but it is the bystanding intelligence of the moral nature and not the outstanding intelligence of thought' (ibid., p. 173). Hence revelation, when it comes to us, does not come to a blank paper. It finds something

[12] London, Hodder and Stoughton (1913).

already present to which it can appeal. He moves towards a concept of reality which reminds us of his own interest in the work of Kant.[13] But we need to go farther than moral statements will take us—beyond the kingdom of conscience to the Kingdom of God. 'The real is neither rational nor ethical, it is redemptive' (ibid., p. 182), and its objective realization is the Cross of Christ, from which, in turn, come the redemptive values which are our key to the historical process and the theological formulations which he defines as 'the intelligible content of the act and person given in the historic revelation' (ibid., p. 212).

Forsyth repudiates the absolutism of the claims of Rome and of 'Socialism', but recognizes that the Church needs more than liberty and search. It needs a creative source of liberty in some fundamental truth or fact. This authoritative basis cannot be in the disputed territory of formulation where heresy and orthodoxy change coats from time to time. Nor can the authority be the expression of majority opinion, as in some political situations, for truth does not change with the casting of votes. There are some things a Church, if it is to be truly a Church, can neither vote away on the plea, 'We have the Spirit of Christ', nor surrender for the sake of a minority of the supposedly élite who claim an inner light. This depositum of the faith, this apostolic word, is not something which the Church is at liberty to vote away. It is given to us by God, not in the form of an infallible Bible nor a complete theology, 'but a continuous act of Gospel, pointed once and present always'.

A difficulty seems to arise about the relationship of the 'Gospel' (by which Forsyth means the act of God and not the account of it), and our assessment of the record of it. On the one hand, the authority of Christ is absolute, and 'no man is a Christian who has not got beyond criticizing his Saviour as such' (ibid., p. 292). But, on the other hand, Forsyth declares that he is only referring to those places where we are agreed what Christ 'said, did and meant' (ibid.) But it so happens that our tendency to credit or not to credit Jesus with particular statements is, to some extent, governed by our individual judgement about what kind of statements could have been uttered by Jesus. Forsyth concedes here that 'we allow for critical reduction in the record, and for his own

---

[13] Cf. Kant, *Metaphysic of Ethics*, tr. Abbott (Longmans), p. 74; 'Morality is the nature of things' (p. 179); 'Our footing is not in process but in purpose' (p. 180).

kenotic self-limitation' (ibid., p. 292). This seems to me to increase Forsyth's difficulties. If we try to define the limits of the authoritative we are in danger of installing our own judgement as the authority. Again, he declares that 'Reason is no authority. It is but the power of discerning authority' (ibid., p. 303). Is he right in supposing that the power of attestation does not convey what we call authority? Or is it correct to assume that anything authoritative can be apprehended by a process of discernment which does not itself possess authority?

In the following chapter, Forsyth returns to his contention that authority is personal and acts on wills. Furthermore, 'as it acts on wills, it must be a will' (ibid., p. 308). (The psychology of the first statement is at variance with his conclusion about the reason, even allowing the piecemeal conception of the mind which was typical of the time, while the second statement involves a curious proposition that all things which act upon the will are themselves wills.)

The final summing-up renews his appeal for a less subjective and individual basis for religion. 'The authority in theology is not external to the matter it works in. It is spiritual. ... It belongs to the revelation itself, not to any voucher which the revelation created, like a book or a church. ... It is an authority objective to us in its source, but subjective in its nature and appeal' (ibid., p. 396). 'The authority is neither primal truth, developed dogma, nor chartered institution, but this act, power and person with whom we have direct dealings' (ibid., p. 398). 'The absoluteness of Christianity is to be sought only in its gospel of grace; treated as the historic act of God for man's moral destiny and not for his scheme of truth' (ibid., p. 399). So it comes about that the Christian can be both critical and submissive. 'The Christian Gospel is an authority for the will, in the will's sphere of history; it is not for the intellect, except so far as the intellect depends on the will. It is an authority which is felt primarily as living, moral majesty, not as truth' (ibid., p. 400). 'The authority is nothing in us, but something in history. It is something given to us. What is in us only recognizes it' (ibid., p. 400).

In spite of defective psychology and a pen so exuberant that frequently the language takes charge of the ideas, Forsyth's work has an evocative and suggestive value. It is apparent that he was trying to direct Christian thinking to a more-nearly objective source of authority. To do this, he points to the Gospel as the act of God, and doing so, anticipates to some extent the insights of Barth and Brunner.

* * *

Martineau[14] is the last of this trio of writers on authority whose works provide a mutually complementary introduction to the present period. He is probably best remembered by moral philosophers as an intuitionist, and his intuitionism plays a considerable part in his study of authority. In the first place, the book considers the seat of authority as distinct from its objective content. The general purpose is clearly stated in the preface: 'If to rest on authority is to mean an acceptance of what, as foreign to my faculty, I cannot know, in mere reliance on the testimony of one who can and does, I certainly find no such basis for religion; inasmuch as second-hand belief, assented to at the dictation of an initiated expert, without personal response of thought and reverence in myself, has no more tincture of religion in it than any other lesson learned by rote. The mere resort to testimony for information beyond our province does not fill the meaning of "authority"; which we never acknowledge till that which speaks to us from another and higher strikes home and wakes the echoes in ourselves, and is thereby instantly transferred from external attestation to self-evidence. And this response it is which makes the moral intuitions, started by outward appeal, reflected back by inward veneration, more than egoistic phenomena; and turning them into correspondency between the universal and the individual mind, invests them with true "authority". We trust in them with awe and inspiration, not with any rationalist arrogance because they are our own, but precisely because they are *not* our own. The *consciousness* of authority is doubtless human; but conditional on the *source* being divine' (ibid., vi–vii).

Martineau sees the outward universe as an act of divine self-abnegation. It is the silence of God, ordered and impersonal. This silence is broken in the moral phenomena of life. The universe may reflect the grandeur and majesty of the supreme cause but to discern more personal attributes we must enter the precincts of humanity. Next, Martineau turns to contemplate human nature and discovers there the power of intuitive moral judgement. This moral perceptiveness he takes to be a gift of God and

[14] *The Seat of Authority in Religion* (Longmans Green), 1890.

to be truly authoritative for our conduct. If we seek the ultimate authority which commands us, we shall not find it where Bentham did, in a mere desire for pleasure or a tendency to avoid pain. At the best, and apart from impulsive action, a calculation about prospective pleasure or pain could only produce an act of prudence. This is the limit beyond which hedonistic motives can never be carried. Hedonism, therefore, reduces all human excellence to prudence. In fact, we feel that a more profound authority lies behind our moral choice and we cannot account for it either in terms of Bentham's theory of the authority of fear or Paley's recourse to the authority of Hell. Nor does he find much evidence for the existence of a so-called 'better self' which could exercise moral authority. Even if such a division of the self existed, the consequences of interaction would belong to the private operations of selfhood and not to society. It has been argued that conscience is simply the influence of the whole over the part, the weight of the moral opinions and attitudes of society pressing upon the life of the individual. But majorities carry no moral authority. 'The highest capital of human wishes, paid up through all the ages, although it may ruin the small dealer in such wares, and drive his venture from the field, can make nothing just that was not just before' (ibid. p. 67). Moral authority is objective to us all and persistently defeats all our efforts to ignore or misrepresent it. 'All minds born into the universe are ushered into the presence of a real righteousness' (ibid., p. 69). Our sense of this authority places us under that which is higher than we are, and we come to see that the word of conscience is the voice of God. Then 'the veil falls from the shadowed face of moral authority, and the directing love of the all-holy God shines forth' (ibid., p. 75).

After his own constructive statement Martineau goes on to examine some spurious claims to authority. He finds both Catholic Church absolutism and Protestant book religion defective. All such claims must be judged by those faculties for appraising authority which are our individual heritage. 'Reason for the rational, conscience for the right—these are the sole organs for appreciating the last claims upon us, the courts of ultimate appeal, whose verdict it is not only weakness, but treason to resist' (ibid., p. 129). Catholic and Protestant alike have shown themselves to be capable of a degree of error which their alleged authority was powerless to check. But denial of absolute authority

THEOLOGY AND AUTHORITY

to hierarchy and canon does not mean they have no authority. It is necessary for us to learn that the power to discern is more important in a Christian than the possession of a corpus of conveyed information. Unalloyed truth does not seem to be within our reach, but this is what men are constantly dreaming of. 'They are afraid of having the water of life spilled, like the rain, upon the meadows, and trickle through the common mould to feed the roots of beauty and of good; and they would store it apart and set it aloft, and secure for it a sacred inclosure to which common men may come for their supply'. So it is that 'the ancient oracle, the medieval church, the Protestant Bible, have been severally detached from the scene and conditions of natural humanity, and regarded as mere media of unerring truth and grace. That this turns out to be a dream of vain desire, that in this world no spot, no body of men, no set of books, can be insulated as the *peculium* of the Holy Spirit, will surprise no one who remembers that, in the weaving of history, two agents are inseparable partners; and that where the pattern is most divine, the web that bears it must still be human' (ibid., p. 289).

Thus it seems, according to Martineau, that so far no objective authority has been found which has anything like the reliability of man's own sensitiveness to moral and spiritual truth. Eventually, when Bible and Church have been laid aside, he finds this authority in what he calls 'the religion of Jesus'. By this term he indicates the picture of Jesus as related to God which remains when we strip away all spurious and mythological elements from the New Testament account. His criteria for achieving this have already been discussed and criticized (pp. 69–70, *supra*). The 'residual' Jesus he discovers by these methods is distinguished from the rest of mankind, not by his knowledge, but by his moral sensitiveness. Hence it would seem that for Martineau the Christian faith resides in a reflexive relationship between the moral sense, as the organ of authority, and God's goodness as revealed to Jesus, as the authoritative object of our moral perceptiveness.

* * *

All these were laudable attempts to erect a modified form of religious authority within the accommodating framework of speculative freedom. But however well they may have dealt with the theoretical problems, they did not exert enough influence to prevent a gradual return to the search for authority in Bible and Church. In 1907 the Roman Catholic Church took firm action against its own more extreme biblical critics. And if that communion needed to safeguard the Bible, how much more was this a necessity to Protestantism. For to the Roman Church the Bible was a secondary authority, dependent upon the defining authority of the Church which fixed the canon of scripture and was still to be regarded as the infallible interpreter of its message. But to the Protestant Church the Bible was a final court of appeal for both doctrine and practice. The reaction towards biblicism within Protestantism could not take a single form because of the heterogeneous nature of the Protestant communions and the multitude of quasi-Protestant sects. The most marked reaction, however, was to be seen in what is called the 'Fundamentalist' attitude (the name comes from the general title of a series of pamphlets published in America in 1909, the purpose of which was to defend biblical orthodoxy against the encroachments of theological liberalism).[15] Biblical literalism has a wide vogue at the present time and no doubt it provides a feeling of religious security for a vast number of Christians who are unable either to accept the authoritarian view of the Church, or to discover a religious *modus vivendi* for themselves without having all its terms dictated from an external source. As though the authority of the Bible, even when so regarded, were still insufficient, at least two influential American sects, the Mormons and the Christian Scientists, have dug up or devised extensive additions to the canon. The Christian Scientists found their addendum to the Bible in the writings of Mary Baker Eddy, and the Mormons were fortunate enough to inherit brand new authoritative scriptures, which were alleged to have been discovered in an American field, in the form of golden tablets (which subsequently disappeared again). The finder, so oddly are these things arranged, was a Mr Smith. But fundamentalism has dangers enough of its own without the addenda. The racialism of the Dutch Reformed Church is said to be of biblicist origin—or perhaps it is of psychological and political origin, but it is defended by the citation of biblical authority; and the segregation of negroes in the southern states of America is advocated on the same grounds.

If this kind of thing were only the refuge of ignorant people it

[15] See Gabriel Hebert, *Fundamentalism and the Church of God* (S.C.M., 1957).

THEOLOGY AND AUTHORITY

would be understandable, and we might hope to be delivered from the implied moral and political dangers by the normal processes of education. But nineteenth-century optimism about the effects of education have not always been fully justified. It is not only the non-educated who seek refuge in authoritarian religion. Sir John Wolfenden expressed concern to a conference held at Oxford (Christmas, 1955), that while the nineteenth-century conflict between science and religion has to a large extent been resolved, there is 'another form of the same disjunction which is current today. It is the antithesis between, on the one hand, the free and fearless ranging of the intellect and, on the other, a neo-obscurantism which takes its start from a literal-minded fundamentalism. ... I am frightened—that is not too strong a word—by the number of young people who today come from sixth forms to Universities with their minds firmly closed, locked, bolted and barred, not just about the Bible and religion in general, but about all sorts of other things as well, philosophy, politics, and history among them. ... And I beg you all to beware lest in tenderness to a naïve form of Christian belief we should be shutting the door on the Holy Spirit of Truth. ... Truth is indivisible, because God is indivisible. ... The operations of the scientific intellect are no less a divinely-inspired activity than the simple beliefs of the immature young' (Quoted by Hebert, ibid., p. 140).

We are compelled to ask why this sort of thing should happen. Why should large numbers of presumably intelligent young people choose a form of religious belief and practice which claims unquestioning assent to an irrational and undigested collection of beliefs, asking only in return the slender apparent verification which comes from the emotional relief of surrendered judgement? The general tendencies which we have reviewed here point to the answer. The search for meaning and purpose in life is renewed in each generation and the seekers are not to be discouraged by the failures or disillusionments of previous generations. But it is a search which can no longer be carried on in the comfortable isolation of a single discipline of thought, with little reference to what is happening elsewhere. In the modern period knowledge has tended, on the one hand, to extreme specialization in the interests of departmental efficiency and, on the other hand, to the kind of overlapping which makes it necessary for the geneticist to listen to the admonitions of the chemist and the chemist, in his turn, to regard with suspicion any laboratory finding which does not satisfy the symmetries of the mathematician. There is a single plateau of knowledge where there used to be a series of mountain peaks related, more or less closely, by their interstitial valleys. This is a great convenience to the sociologist who wishes to take an excursion over the territories of epidemiology or genetics or criminology in order to pursue and relate his own discoveries. He will, in fact, discover that it is possible to walk from one end to the other of the formidable plateau with only a few areas of marshland to indicate where the deep valleys once ran. If, however, anyone should seek to nourish and propagate a religious belief in a life which will be in daily contact with this interrelated system, he must adopt one of two courses. Either he must set his new belief apart on a lonely pinnacle and seek to reconcile the apparent conflicts between religion and the other branches of knowledge by the curious notion of a double truth, or he can lay his faith on the commonwealth of the plateau and see what happens to it. If intelligent and otherwise educated young people are really choosing the former course, it would be interesting to know under what inner compulsions they act. Outbreaks of irrationalism are not uncommon in civilized society, but their occurrence can never be ignored without risking the integrity of the whole social structure. This observation should rank as a truism in the face of the activities of modern political authoritarianism.

If there are numbers of people who are going to the biblical literalists and their kin and asking for dogmatic instruction, there must surely be as many or more who find their respite from the secular-sacred conflict in a revived concept of ecclesiastical authority. The past century has seen many Anglicans of stature, from Newman to Knox, bending backward to Rome, and a far greater number staying within Anglicanism to work toward a renascence of catholic authority. To a certain extent, this movement toward a more catholic conception of churchmanship, which has affected even the more markedly Protestant Churches, was a necessary correction of laxity in discipline and in the ordering of worship. Canon E. C. Rich's *Spiritual Authority in the Church of England*[16] traces the steps by which the authority of Rome was replaced in England by the primary Anglican concept of the

[16] Longmans Green, 1953.

authority of scripture and tradition. This position was challenged by various theological repercussions of the changing philosophical climate. Chillingworth, for instance, decided that reason was the final arbiter in matters of scriptural interpretation, and this apparent sensitiveness to the growing influence of rationalism was followed, at the appropriate time, by an empiricistic deflection to a more experimental type of theology. Experimentalism gave place, in due course, to the extreme individualism of the Quaker. But at this point even the Quaker had to resort to the confirmatory authority of the Quaker fellowship. 'Here then, we discern, even in the most radical and individualistic of Puritans, a sense that the Church *in some form or other* is a necessary accompaniment of spirituality' (Rich, ibid., p. 58).

This discovery has been made all over again in modern Christianity, and the individualistic and independent era is being followed by a mood more favourable to much that is implied by the word 'churchmanship'. Ecumenicity is an important and prominent feature of the Church of the twentieth century, and while some Christians meditate on the need for greater unity others have come together to mend some at least of the scattered and broken fragments of the Church. Wherever this happens the resultant communion appears to move towards the 'higher' and consequently more authoritarian point of view represented in the uniting bodies. We record this without comment as one more indication of a general tendency in the development of the modern Church.

It is easy to see why reaction has taken place. Christian liberalism was essentially destructive. 'The Liberal divine is in his element when he is deflating obscurantism and tripping up blind guides; when he is standing for freedom from the pretensions of an intransigent or corrupt authority. But when all authority has been laid low, including the ultimate authority which can alone give freedom its sanction and responsibility, ' "now the day is over" for the Liberal, and the "night is drawing nigh".'[17] Dr Vidler is of the opinion that the critical task is finished: 'Freedom to believe and say what you think has been won . . . we can be as independent as we please. The question now is whether there is any authority or law or God in the world and over the world, on which we can depend, in which we can trust, to whom we are responsible, whom

[17] A. R. Vidler, *Essays in Liberality* (S.C.M., 1957), p. 18.

we can know and love' (ibid., p. 18). But if authority is to be re-erected on the understandable plea that we must have some sort of authority or perish, there may be need of more and more critical minds in and about religion to ensure that the proposed new authority is not one which will ultimately bind the spirit of man with his old fetters and make of all our vaunted modern freedom an evanescent episode in the long night of tutelage.

It is only fair to say that the Church-centred tendency we have just mentioned has now found widespread acceptance among Christian thinkers who could hardly be described as reactionary. Dr Leonard Hodgson, for instance, regards this new evaluation of the Church as 'the outcome of developing the critical methods of the theology of my youth'.[18] From an ecclesiastical point of view Christianity has been re-appraised as 'the faith of the original disciples of Jesus Christ', who after His resurrection became conscious of themselves as 'the new and true Israel, the Christian ecclesia' (ibid., pp. 19-20). It is not difficult to see how this line of thought can lead to the conclusion that Christianity is, when rightly regarded, 'the faith of the Church', and if that step is taken, it would seem to involve consequences for the Church's authority. We should, of course, have to be fairly certain about the identity of the Church before much progress could be made along this line. Up to the present this is still a matter on which there is wide disagreement.

* * *

We have not made any mention of the general theological tendency which is indicated by the term 'Biblical Theology'. This tendency, which is perhaps the most influential aspect of Protestant theology at the present time, and has not been without influence on Catholic thought, is too widespread to be called a school. The theologian who approaches his task with this outlook regards the content of Holy Scripture as the data of his investigation. He may, indeed, regard it as a theological impropriety to look elsewhere for his material. This means that the actual message of the Bible has become again an object for close study, and that the Bible is being conceived in the new sense suggested by Barth's conception of 'the Word of God'. Theologians who share this widely held point of view are intent to hear, beyond the mere

[18] *For Faith and Freedom*, Gifford Lectures (Oxford, Blackwell, 1956), I.22.

record of events and sayings, and far beyond the long scrutiny of text and origin, an authentic proclamation of God.

The authenticity of this 'word' is not impaired seriously by the human limitations which are evident when the Bible is investigated as history or literature. The Bible is accepted for what it most obviously is, a book written by men, with its own share of the general fallibility of artefacts. But, as Brunner has pointed out, it is a human book because that is the necessary pre-condition if it is to be, for us who are limited to a human viewpoint, a divine book. The Bible is, in this latter sense, an activity of God, and its central message is that 'the Word became flesh and dwelt among us'. While the passion of Christ receives a great deal of attention from Barth, the general events of his life are less central, and even his suffering and death are thought to obscure the setting forth of the plain truth of God. Christ the man is, to some extent, the concealer of God. It is the risen Christ who reveals God and who discloses the meaning of the suffering and humiliation which bore such a human aspect.

This is pre-eminently a theology of revelation, which finds its authority in the self-communication of God which comes to the faithful as an overtone of the word of scripture. This view of the nature of the authority in religion is not unlike that put forward by Forsyth, whose writings have consequently received renewed attention.

From this type of theology there has also proceeded a negative result of some interest to the present study. Good followers of Barth have been inclined to regard only the revelatory type of theology as in any sense valid, and have condemned philosophical theology, or the attempt to progress towards theological truth by rational means and from premises other than those supplied by revelation, as suspect, or even sinful. Theological positivism of this sort will have nothing to do with the suggestion that there can be any such thing as 'an ascent, by the natural light of reason, through created things to the knowledge of God. . .'[19] Rather does it follow Luther in his repudiation of the natural theology of the scholastics, while admitting to the same condemnation not only the rationalism of the eighteenth-century Deists, but the whole body of speculative theology which flourished in the

---

[19] St Thomas Aquinas, *Summa Contra Gentiles*, IV, Chap. 1, quoted by Dr John Baillie, *The Idea of Revelation in Recent Thought* (Oxford, 1956).

nineteenth century and produced feebler echoes in the twentieth.

Behind this movement there lies a new conception of revelation. 'What is offered to man's apprehension in any specific revelation is not truth concerning God but the living God Himself.'[20] The Christian, according to this view, is not provided with a supply of guaranteed truths, but with a contact with God, and with the fact of Divine self-impartation. Both the word of scripture and the dogmas of the Church are human words, but they are about divine events, and so they have a content which is beyond the reach of the unaided human intelligence.

Barth's condemnation of so-called natural theology was uttered in the interest of a new and much more realistic attitude to the Bible, but it was also an echo of Kant's verdict upon the philosophical search for proofs of the existence of God. Kant decided that reason, in its purely speculative role, was quite incapable of proving the existence of a supreme being. So, of course, is the Bible. But that does not prevent us from inquiring whether there are communications of divine origin which are given to the world through the minds of men. If there are such communications, they obviously cannot come other than through human minds, for we know of no other channel of information. Biblical revelation has had to use the fallible human intellect. If the difference be only in subject matter then the Barthian position is secure, but this does not seem to be the case. Much of the biblical record, especially in the Old Testament, is more remarkable for its point of view than for any striking peculiarity or uniqueness in the events which are reported. This is recognized in Dr Baillie's book (p. 64); '... the receiving is as necessary to a completed act of revelation as the giving. It is only so far as the action of God in history is understood as God means it to be understood that revelation has place at all. The illumination of the receiving mind is a necessary condition of the divine self-disclosure'. He finds general agreement about this among contemporary theologians and cites Barth, Temple and Brunner. But if it is divine illumination which makes the work of the prophet and witness significant, may not the same illumination operate in the mind of a metaphysician as he contemplates, so far as he is able, the totality of given experience? This is taken for granted in the quotation from Dr Temple which follows (Baillie, op. cit., p. 70). 'Unless all

[20] Temple, *Nature, Man and God*, p. 322, quoted Baillie, op. cit., p. 33.

existence is a medium of revelation, no particular revelation is possible. . . . Either all occurrences are in some degree revelation of God, or else there is no such revelation at all; for the conditions of the possibility of any revelation require that there should be nothing which is not revelation.' Dr Temple did not, of course, share Barth's view about the impossibility of a valid philosophical approach to theology.

We have noted this retreat from speculative theology because it seems to belong to the more general tendency to look for a new and more acceptable form of authority to replace ecclesiastical absolutism or biblical literalism for the benefit of those to whom neither of these is acceptable. We must also note that in recent years the inevitable reaction has taken place, and that a number of the most able theological minds are rediscovering the compatibility of revelation with the thought-world to which they are introduced by their own speculative endeavours, as well as by the attitude of mind and heart which is the product of a tolerant and curious conspectus of the broad content of the philosophy of the past. In this connexion it has been pointed out by Paul Tillich that theological discussion cannot in fact disengage itself from a wide range of philosophical terms and concepts which it tends to take for granted. 'The Bible itself always uses the categories and concepts which describe the structure of experience. On every page of every religious or theological text these concepts appear: time, space, cause, thing, subject, nature, movement, freedom, necessity, life, value, knowledge, experience, being and non-being. Biblicism may try to preserve their popular meaning, but then it ceases to be theology. It must neglect the fact that a philosophical understanding of these categories has influenced ordinary language for many centuries. . . . The theologian must take seriously the meaning of the terms he uses. They must be known to him in the whole depth and breadth of their meaning. Therefore, the systematic theologian must be a philosopher in critical understanding even if not in creative power.'[21]

The mention of Tillich brings existentialism to mind, for his own theological systematizations are obviously indebted to the ontological concepts of Heidegger, and though Heidegger may have expressed a preference to be called an ontologist, he is more easily understood within the framework of existentialism. It

[21] *Systematic Theology* (Nisbet), I.24-5.

is with the existentialist type of theology that we shall be concerned rather than with the existentialism which, in a secular setting, is sometimes a philosophy and sometimes a temper or frame of mind. Even theological existentialism presents a great variety of facets, for Martin Buber is Jewish, Gabriel Marcel is Roman Catholic, Berdyaev is of the Eastern Orthodox Church, and Bultmann and Karl Jaspers have a Protestant background.

Before we seek any apparent connexion between existentialist theology and the problem of authority it may be well to say something about the theological import of the movement. In the form in which it appears in the work of Bultmann, who is probably the most important of the theologians whose philosophical background is of this kind, it represents a shifting of interest from the transcendentalism of Barth to the human predicament of man himself. If God is to be found, He will be found inside the limitations of the human situation. It is perfectly clear, at any rate, that if He is only to be found outside these limitations, He will not be found by us. The existentialism in terms of which Bultmann understands the teaching of the Bible, and in terms of which he believes it can best be reinterpreted, is the analytic and ontological variety expounded by Heidegger. This existential analytic is a descriptive analysis of what is revealed to man in his own self-disclosure as existing. Such a field of observation is thought to be more fruitful for the study of the special problems of man as an individual being, including the problems of religion, than the merely objective procedures of science. Science, according to this view, is adequate to deal with an objective world, and properly so employed. But the objects of its study are no more than objective. They exist in the bare sense that they are extant (for this bare existence Heidegger uses the term *Vorandenheit*). Man, however, is more than an object of study; he is capable of uniting the objective and the subjective in his own person. This unique mode of being is implied in the term *Existenz* as Heidegger uses it. This is the object of study for the existentialist, but it is to some extent also the subject who undertakes the study. Knowledge may presumably be correlated, but access to it is at least as individual as it was for Descartes.

If we view the implications of this type of philosophical theology against the background of the authoritarian—anti-authoritarian dialectic which has been put into profile in this survey, the result is interesting. It is clear that one of the most propulsive influences behind the movement is the urge to reinstate the individual at a time in the development of world society when he is in danger of submersion. Existentialism, moreover, 'by insisting on the individual, on the free subject, is also a protest against the general tendency in our civilization to resolve the individual into his social function or functions, such as tax-payer, voter, civil servant, engineer, trade unionist, etc. This theme has been developed by Gabriel Marcel in particular, who believes that the tendency towards the functionalization of man involves a degradation of the human person'.[22] It is difficult to see how a theological movement with this background can be other than opposed to religious authoritarianism, whatever else it may be, and this will be true whether the authoritarianism is of the ecclesiastical or biblical variety. In Bultmann, for instance, there is an attitude to the Bible which is much more liberal than that of biblical theology. He is curiously eager to rid the record of all its mythological content, but he still finds in the Bible an authentic word of God to man, more and not less authentic because it is also man's word about himself. This is possible because 'In religious faith, God is disclosed immediately with the self and the world.'[23]

The individualism of the existential approach has laid it open to the charge of excessive subjectivism. The same charge is obviously invited by existential theology. The knowledge of God of which it speaks is existential: it is not a set of propositions about God, but the knowledge which is implicit in our faith in God (ibid., p. 56). It is the cricketer's own knowledge of the game rather than the deliverances of Wisden. But surely this is the familiar claim of the mystics and pietists to possess an inner light, a peculiar and private revelation of the will of God which is not subject to external authority? The difference, and it is all-important, is that the existentialist makes no claim to a superior revelation of truth which is authoritative for other men. The discovery of truth is individual and private, according to him, but it is not necessarily reserved for the special insight of the few, or necessarily consequent upon the enjoyment of some kind of experience which only selected people are likely to enjoy. The experience in which the vital facts about man and his world are given (and about God, too,

[22] *Contemporary Philosophy*, Frederic Copleston (Burns and Oates, 1956).
[23] *An Existentialist Theology*, John Macquarrie (S.C.M., 1955), p. 62.

if you are minded to go so far) is the individual possession of all men.

While there are many shades of opinion within the borders of theistic existentialism, there would seem to be a common consent that the individual is free from the impositions of external authority, whether it is the authority of science which seeks to objectify and limit the self, or the authority of religious systems which not only define the goal of the self, but insist that they shall be permitted to dictate the steps by which the goal is to be reached. In the face of that the individual cannot be other than free, for freedom is his human lot and distinction. 'I am the possibility of my own being, in the sense that I am never something already made, something finished and classifiable: I am constantly creating myself, as it were, or freely realizing my being through my own choices'[24]

The debate continues, of course. Barthianism has very wide attachments, especially in the Reformed theology of Europe and in America. Fundamentalism persists in varying degrees with tenacious attachments to the differing theologies which biblical literalism produces (from the theology of Evangelical Anglicanism to that of the Seventh Day Adventists). The Liberals who remain undilutedly liberal seem either to have crept into corners or to have banded together in small groups—such as the Modern Churchman's Union. Summarizing his own experience of the theology of the present century, Dr Hodgson writes: 'The political convulsions of this century have produced in many quarters scepticism of the capacity of human reason to discover truth' (op. cit., I.22). If our reading of history has been at all a fair one, the reason which Hodgson gives for the rise of neo-orthodoxy is too narrow. Perhaps it would be truer to say that the upheavals of the present century have precipitated the crisis by provoking a deeply-felt longing for the anchorage of a given certainty in religion. However, to resume Dr Hodgson's summing up of his first lecture, the situation has also produced 'a desire for a religion proclaiming an authoritative revelation of God which does not submit to man's judgement but simply demands his acceptance and obedience, for a theology which confines itself to the exposition of the revealed truth (ibid.). In the discussion which follows we are to consider, from a philosophical or critical viewpoint, whether the rôle of authority in religion can be regarded as thus categorical and absolute.

[24] Copleston, op. cit., p. 160. He is summarizing the views of Jaspers.

CHAPTER SIX

A CRITIQUE OF RELIGIOUS AUTHORITY

IT MIGHT be well to begin this section with a word or two about viewpoint. A 'philosophical or critical' viewpoint was proposed at the end of the previous chapter. In this case that does not signify an adherence to any school of philosophy. There may be philosophical inclinations in most of us, and we can hardly hope to be without biases, but philosophical loyalties are out of place. So if there should be discovered in what follows an undue susceptibility to the influence of existentialism, or a nostalgia for nineteenth-century idealism, or an apparent devotion to Hegelian dialectic, it is all blissfully unconscious. We would require that the notion of open-mindedness be counted as an integral part of the meaning of 'philosophical'. None of us, however, can be openminded about everything, as Descartes found. We have to have our house to live in while we are doing our knocking down and rebuilding. This is especially true with regard to matters which are concerned with religion. As well as possessing finely shaded or broad, impromptu opinions on the subject of religion, or opinions of an intermediate kind, all of us who live in a Christian civilization are either Christians or non-Christians. If we are to write about religion at all, therefore, we must do it from our side of the fence, and to do that is to lay oneself open to the charge of prejudice. When Lord Russell has written about religion, especially since his general views have become well known, he can hardly have hoped that religious people would take very much notice of his opinions; they know how firmly he is planted on the other side of the fence. But he would have been entitled to expect that they would examine his arguments.

The following chapters are written with only such an expectation. The point of view is detached so far as one can be detached about religion. Kemp Smith began his introduction to Hume's *Dialogues Concerning Natural Religion* (Nelson Edn, 1947) with these words: 'Hume's writings on religion are composed—this is at once their strength and weakness—from the standpoint of a detached observer.' But Hume was scarcely a detached observer where religion was concerned. He was repelled by the religion he had seen as a child and found it impossible to believe the doctrines in which the Christian faith was presented to him. A later passage in Kemp Smith's introduction states that 'Once he had succeeded in formulating the general lines of his own philosophy, he had quite definitely concluded that religion is not merely an ambiguous but in the main a *malign* influence' (p. 11). This is not what one would regard as detachment. Perhaps one can be as detached as that while believing that the Christian faith is fundamentally benign, but that its beliefs and formulations are not to be excluded from the critical investigation which is to be accorded to any claim to possess knowledge, or to be in some way able to declare what is true. This, at any rate, is the viewpoint from which these chapters are to be written, so that they cannot take the form of a theological discourse, although terms like 'the Word of God' and 'revelation' may be employed in their theological sense.

SOME SUGGESTED DEFINITIONS OF AUTHORITY

At this point it may do something to simplify our later discussion if we consider a few suggested definitions of authority. The first group of definitions come from a work published for the American Society of Political and Legal Philosophy.[1] C. J. Friedrich defines authority as 'the potentiality of reasoned elaboration' (p. 35). He believes that the ancient connotations of the word '*auctoritas*' support him in assuming its semi-rational character and he is concerned to dissociate authority from power. Authority is to be understood by considering relationships like those of parent and child, or teacher and pupil, where we recognize a rational claim to be believed. This 'potentiality of reasoned elaboration' Friedrich takes to refer to a quality of communication rather than of persons or institutions. 'Such communications, whether opinions or commands, are not demonstrated through rational discourse', but they have a potential rationality, they are 'worthy of acceptance' (p. 35). 'When we speak of the authority of a person we are using a shorthand expression to indicate that he possesses the capacity to issue authoritative communications' (pp. 35–6).

Dr Arendt's essay in the same work is distinguished by a careful

---

[1] *Authority*, ed. Carl J. Friedrich (Harvard, 1958).

treatment of the historical background of the word '*auctoritas*'. She regards authority as a non-Greek concept. Plato sought to invest the laws with the power of the despot, the ruler of the house, and he dreamed of a philosopher-king who would embody reason and rule in his own person, but any authority which the rules or the ruler might possess would have to be based upon ultimate principles which were not themselves man-made. The natural conclusion, which Plato himself seems to have avoided, was that 'neither man nor a god is the measure of all things, but the good itself' (ibid., p. 93). Aristotle, on the other hand, sought imperfect, pre-political analogies, such as the relationship of father and child, master and slave, or young and old, as a base upon which to erect the notion of a division of society into rulers and ruled. The origin of the Roman *Auctoritas*, however, was purely political. It was centred on the uniqueness of the city itself, and directed backward in reverence toward the act of foundation. *Auctoritas* is that which augments the foundation of the city. This exaggerated respect for the past led to the Roman view that 'growth was directed towards the past' (p. 101), and their view of the past was enlarged to include not only the roman foundation, but the wide range of their cultural and intellectual heritage from Greece.

We have taken over the theory of authority and tradition, but without experiencing the politico-philosophical conflict which was its background in Greece, or the experience of foundation on which Roman religion, authority and tradition were based (p. 102). The Roman notion of the conjunction of authority and foundation was incorporated in the way the Christian Church treated its source material, and Christianity was able to add a genuinely transcendent authority-revelation.

Bertrand de Jouvenal also offers a definition of authority in the same work. He seeks to present the situation in which authority is exercised in its simplest form: A formulates an imperative statement and B complies. To an observer, A's statement appears to be an efficient imperative. This relationship of bidding and complying falls within the field of suggestion and response, but it must be distinguished from the bargaining relationship which contains a rational element. Such bidding and complying is unrelated to contractual arrangements, it is a phenomenon of human nature, and is *sui generis*. Nor need there be fear of consequences to compel compliance. There are, however, cases of derived authority where uniforms or trappings impress subjects who are suitably conditioned. But if we can divest A of trappings and he still obtains B's compliance, that is a pure relation of authority. This relation is 'the fundamental element upon which the whole complex fabric of society is reared' (p. 161).

De Jouvenal discards the notion that members of a State originally learnt to comply from fear of punishment, for who would have conceded the power to punish? Rather than examine the imaginary prehistory of the State we should examine power relationships at work now. We see this in the formation of any association where, as must be the case, one individual takes the initiative and prevails upon others to join him. This is a relation of pure authority. Human society is necessarily a conflict of authorities, for under the dominant authority there must be room for people who have 'the naked capacity of mustering assent'.

In the concluding essay of the work, E. A. Hoebel (p. 222), approaching the subject from an anthropological point of view, defines authority as 'the explicit capacity to direct the behaviour of others'. He notices this capacity even in infra-human primates. The wide range of potential behaviour in man, coupled with the long period of post-natal development during which he is unable to choose the forms of behaviour which are generally advantageous to him, makes it necessary for childhood to suffer authoritative control. Further, successful group life requires that modes of behaviour be selected which are not mutually harmful. Selection itself requires acts of decision, and this is an exercise of authority. Hoebel advances the view that the type of authority likely to be recognized in a simple society depends upon the dominant activity or need of the society. In a food-seeking community leadership would rest upon qualities like skill in hunting, while in cases where the relationship of effort and result is less clear, the ascription of supernatural influence invests a leader with authority. Generally, 'Authority rests on an intimate and superior knowledge of how best to exploit the meagre resources of the local ecology' (p. 227). Some such system of authority seems to be necessary for biological and cultural survival. It begins with child training, but in later life it depends, primitively, upon achievement and personal qualities. Systems of succession tend to blur this evident and meaningful choice, though in complex primitive societies authority is allowed to practice polygamy so that there is no automatic succession but a relatively large choice. It is difficult to avoid the conviction that there is a good deal of truth in this account of the rise of authority in simple societies, and difficult not to feel the probability of the inference that some of the simple and original elements of our own relationships of authority are similar in their origin and nature. The fundamental relationship of authority seems to be that of parent and child. There can be no doubt that it preceded all other social relationships, though not consciously, for the group of families is itself an instinctive association at all levels of animal behaviour. At this most primitive level two possible authority-bestowing factors are clear: submission to parents and the recognition of some sort of excellence or superiority in other members of the group. Similarly, if we take cognizance of the tabulations of instinctive endowment which emerge from the studies of the psychologists, we will notice certain commonly recognized innate factors in human behaviour which have a bearing upon the authority relationship. From the side of the one who is subject to authority, the relevant endowments are those concerned with nutrition, escape, and submission; while from the other side, the corresponding endowments are those which are concerned with parental care and with self-display or self-assertion. It would not matter, for this mode of interpretation, whether we adopted the older schemes of instinct or propensity tabulation, like that of McDougall, or newer forms which simplify the inherited 'biological imperatives' and regard impulses such as those to dominate or to submit as social derivatives.[2] Even if our psychological viewpoint inclines us to classify people in terms of types of response, rather than endowment, the same broad distinctions seem to emerge, and we find at one end of the response scale the expansive type, rebellious and dominating, and at the other end the recessive or self-effacing type, whose inclination is to find a leader and follow him.

This broad type-division has been studied empirically among American kindergarten children and the study revealed that some children meet a situation of deprivation by almost unvaried pleading, whilst others respond to a similar situation by attempting to dominate.[3]

[2] Cf. Kimball Young, *Handbook of Social Psychology*, 5th Edn. (Routledge and Kegan Paul, London, 1953), pp. 80-5.
[3] See the account given in Kimball Young, ibid., pp. 224ff.

The indications are very strong that there really is a submissive tendency in human nature, so that it is of the greatest importance that we should be aware of it and make due allowance for its effect, whether we are considering those who seek to wield authority over their fellows or those who find themselves commanded by it. A. C. Garnett puts the matter like this: 'Under certain conditions human beings simply *want* to submit themselves to leadership, guidance and control. They follow gladly and find a real satisfaction in following the leader.... To exhibit strong attachment to a leader or to a cause, and complete submission of self in loyalty to him or it, is universally recognized as a sign of strength, not of weakness.'[4] Garnett assumes that the feelings of submission which are normally awakened by the group or herd are also awakened by the dominant member of the group, who acts as a symbol of the group.

The common factor in these descriptive analyses of human endowment is something very much like the simple egoism of Hobbes. So far as one can see, the only endowment we have which is non-egoistic is that which impels us to care for our young. But this parental impulse combines very easily with the self-regarding urge to win security by domination. The other side of our nature exhibits a different type of response to environmental perils. It is a submissive response, but not for that reason less defensive. Submission is the way of concealment in society, it is the way of undemanding alliance with the strong and the wise, and it may be chosen by the majority of men for reasons concerned with their own physical or mental endowment, or simply because, in a social universe of intense competition, it is more likely to produce the desired end of security than the method of domination.

All that we can learn from this material is the approximate nature of the impulses to seek and submit to authority, or to seek and wield it, which appear to be part of our nature. Even if we can be satisfied that such primary impulses do exist, we shall have learnt only a little about what is understood by the term 'authority', but that little may be of great importance. If there is an instinctive basis of the kind suggested, we must allow for the survival of an irrational content in authority, and we must expect

---

[4] *The Mind in Action*, Contemporary Library of Psychology (Nisbet and Cambridge University Press, 1931), p. 111.

that such a content will exist at a high emotional potential, and will be almost ineradicable.

*   *   *

From all these suggestions it is possible to begin to build up a fairly comprehensive notion of what people are talking about when they use the word 'authority'. None of the suggested definitions, however, is particularly concerned with religious authority, though Dr Arendt did relate her definition to the authority of the Church. We shall need not only to discuss these notions of authority, but to move forward to the question of authority in religion. We will need to know whether it can be assumed that 'authority' is used in religion in a sense cognate with its extra-religious use. Otherwise we may be guilty of outlining a general picture of authority which is sufficiently descriptive of parental authority or political authority, but not of religious authority.

If we look a little more carefully at the accounts of authority which have been given so far, it is obvious that they are to some extent mutually destructive. Friedrich's insistence upon the concealed rational content of authority appears to be at odds with the simple imperatival relationship which De Jouvenal indicates as the model and source of authority. Hoebel's anthropological approach is one of which De Jouvenal is very critical, but the definition which he reaches is very much like that of De Jouvenal. Dr Arendt's concept of authority is essentially retrospective, while De Jouvenal insists that the right answers are more likely to be reached by a study of simple authority relationships in the present. Perhaps the different conclusions which one can reach concerning authority are to be explained by the differences which are possible in our approach to the subject. If we suppose that the basic human relationship is pre-social and that the characteristics of the relationship change with the circumstances and nature of the societies or associations which developed later, we may be able to suggest a scheme which would to some extent unify these definitions.

Since we may presume that individual relationships existed prior to any organized society, it is reasonable to look first for an explanation in terms of individual psychology, and within the simplest, that is to say the least sophisticated, forms of human behaviour in inter-personal association. If there are indeed differing tendencies in individuals which incline them to react in fundamentally different ways when they encounter the challenge or competition of other individuals, if some individuals react by seeking to dominate while others react submissively, then this process is likely to influence the formation of relationships at the most uncomplicated and primitive level. Just as one kitten in the litter tends to dominate by its liveliness and strength, so some men differ from their fellows in natural qualities and will tend to dominate their immediate human environment, while others will find their security by submitting and sheltering under the qualities of the dominators. As social relationships grow more complex, the qualities needed to command authority will become more and more varied to meet the requirements of new group activities and more involved relationships. In the hunting community, for instance, an unusual endowment of strength will not suffice to equip the leader, and qualities of subtlety, agility, acuity of vision and hearing, and tenacity of purpose will become necessary if any individual is to dominate his fellows. When group clashes begin to occur some of the hunter's qualities may stand him in good stead, but the qualities needed for the good hunter will probably need to be supplemented by some enhanced powers of organization and by a keener appreciation of the probable behaviour of human enemies, if the hunting leader is to become a warrior leader. In later and more sophisticated societies the authority of the leader may no longer be able to rest upon the skills and aptitudes which made his warrior or hunter forefather outstanding. For the sake of the stability of society there may need to be an agreed mode of transmitting authority from father to son, or some more or less artificial mode of selection, because succession which depends on free competition of qualities would not be practicable in a large and fairly complex society. This is the stage which saw the emergence of monarchy, and the basis is still irrational, but in the course of further development in the direction of representative government it is evident that certain rational criteria would begin to assert themselves. The leadership of a group or of an appointed or elected individual would tend to rest upon a claim and admission of qualities of leadership, among which would have to be included knowledge of a kind which would fit the prospective member of the government to understand the problems of his society and to be at least likely to find solutions for them.

The kind of evolution we have indicated would exhibit authority in a different light at different stages of development. At the more primitive levels, the crude factor of power would be likely to predominate; in a hereditary system men would learn to look to the past for the reason or cause which had constituted present society, while in a democratic system there would be a presumption that an authority erected for rational purposes would exercise the power of rational direction, so that its directives could be expected to possess 'the potentiality of reasoned elaboration'.

This, of course, does not pretend to be an exhaustive account of the development of different stages of authority—nor is it novel. But if it is even broadly true, it does account for the survival of differing accounts and conceptions of authority. Indeed, we might go farther than that to assert that the varied bases of authority, which we considered to have arisen during successive periods of the history of society, coexist in modern society; so that when we speak of the relationships of authority now we may be referring to a range of similar imperatival or coercive relationships which exact obedience in much the same way, but whose bases are not in all cases the same. Hence we might expect to find one type of authority still based upon tradition, others whose basis is some sort of power, and others whose basis is to some extent rational. Nor would this exhaust the possible bases, because authority might well still be based upon any quality or property or attribution of quality which men have at any time regarded as worthy of respect or obedience, or for some other reason authoritative.

It is of interest here that Max Weber distinguishes three types of legitimate authority: legal rational authority, traditional authority, and charismatic authority.[5] The distinction is made between them according to the grounds on which their respective claims to validity rest. These are, first, rational grounds, resting on belief in the 'legality' of a pattern of normative rules, and the right of those elevated to authority under those rules to issue commands; second, traditional grounds, resting on the established belief in the sanctity of customs originating in the past and in the legitimacy of the status of those who exercise authority under them; and thirdly, charismatic grounds, resting on an appraisal of special qualities of sanctity or heroism or exemplary character in an individual, and of the normative pattern of behaviour so revealed

[5] *Theory of Economic and Social Organization* (William Hodge and Co.), pp. 121ff.

or ordained. None of these, Weber warns us, are likely to be found in pure form.

There is no need for us to examine or try to criticize Weber's scheme. Its use here is illustrative. It illustrates in another way what was indicated by the divergent views that we have already noticed. There is apparently no single basis for authority and types of authority which have developed from different bases appear now to coexist and to continue to function in the regulation of society. What we shall need to do now is to inquire first, whether in spite of its multiform basis, 'authority' signifies only one type of relationship or many differing ones: and second, whether authority which owes its power to a specific basis may with propriety be allowed to operate in matters where that particular basis is not strictly relevant.

Are we then to think of one kind of relationship when we speak of authority? On the whole it would clarify our thinking if we did so. However the forms and trappings of authority and the bases of authority may have changed and developed, whenever we use the word 'authority' thoughtfully we must be aware of its primary reference to a simple relationship of effective command and compliance—the 'efficient imperative' of De Jouvenal. De Jouvenal, in fact, was defining in terms of the actual relationship as we know it, whereas Arendt, Friedrich, and Hoebel, with their respective concerns for tradition, potential rationality, and primitive power to direct behaviour, were looking at some of the grounds upon which the relationship may be founded. It is incidental, though interesting, that the grounds they distinguish happen to resemble so closely those distinguished by Weber.

It may be objected, against the essentially unitary view that is proposed, that it fails to take account, for instance, of the authority of the scientist in his own field. Is it not true to say that this is not only an authority upon a particular basis, the basis of specialised knowledge and rational ability, but also an authority which is different as a relationship? And what of an expression like, 'The authority of the facts'? Is that a justifiable use of the word 'authority' and does it imply some sort of imperatival relationship? It is true that we use the word 'authority' to describe an effect of the knowledge and wisdom of, *inter alios*, a scientist of eminence. It is doubtful, however, whether the relationship of a scientist to scientists, where it is rationally conceived, is strictly one of authority, and where it is of authority it is not scientific. If Sir William Farigrade should tell his fellow scientists of the existence of a universal elastic medium called 'aether', they will not, as scientists, believe him because of his eminence, or his learning, or his deep honesty of purpose, any more than they would believe him because he is a good husband and a lover of Bach—although they may be *inclined* to believe him, and if so we should say that they are experiencing a relationship of authority. They will require, sooner or later, to examine the evidence upon which his findings are based. Of course, scientists, as human beings, are sometimes swayed by the opinions of eminent members of their discipline, and they are then experiencing an effect of authority, but one would think that they are not then acting in their strictly scientific capacity. Needless to say, Sir William's opinions about outer space will be accepted with uncritical alacrity by a great number of people who are not scientists, and they too will be deferring to authority. So we should conclude that when a scientist exerts authority, in this refined sense as a generator of a coercive or imperatival relationship, he is not acting scientifically. Nevertheless, we must accept such a use of the word so long as it is borne in mind that it is a metaphorical use.

If this is the case, when we ascribe authority intra-scientifically, to the work of a particular individual, we simply mean to say that the findings of such a man need to be considered with greater than usual care before we can set them aside, or that we are aware that his utterances on subjects relevant to his field of study are backed by greater knowledge and ability than is commonly the case, and therefore are more likely to be correct.

The expression 'the authority of the facts' is similarly metaphorical. It indicates an attitude of reliance upon empirical data which is completely contrary to the attitude which seeks to be directed by authority, or is content to accept the direction of authority. In any investigation, however, if we find ourselves confronted by a set of relevant facts, they give an inclination to our conclusion about the matter under investigation, but this is a rational process, and not recourse to authority. Such uses, then, are metaphorical.

We can take it, then, that the 'authority' of the expert is partly a metaphorical use of the word, and purely metaphorical within the proprieties of his own discipline, for there his communications must ultimately be judged by their content and not by their source. Similarly, such expressions as 'the authority of the facts' use the word as a device of communication to indicate the persuasive or compulsive force of evidence.

Now it so happens that both these instances of the use of the word 'authority' are concerned with truth. It appears to be true that the deliverances of authority, as the word is generally used, are of two sorts. According to our sketch of the probable development of the authority relationship, and the psychological factors which we noticed as probably fundamental to the relationship, the primary and original function of authority is to command. This is almost, one would think, beyond cavil, and the majority of the definitions and divisions of authority which we have noticed bear a sense which would support this view. But authority has also been claimed by persons and organizations who have not been content to say to us, 'Don't kill my deer', or 'Drive on the left', but have declared, and often of matters on which our knowledge was uncertain, 'This is true'.

It is understandable that the simple relationship of authority, the imperatival relationship which, we have suggested, underlies most of our thinking about authority, should easily pass over into a claim of right concerning truth telling or truth knowing. The leader who has gained by his personal qualities, or by some inheritance, an ascendancy over his group, so that his commands in practical matters are obeyed without question, is hardly likely to be modest and uncommanding when questions of knowledge arise within his domain. If he is the oracle who must be obeyed when the question arises, 'What shall we do?', he can hardly hope to maintain his authority should he plead ignorance in the face of the inevitable question, 'What shall we believe about X?' What seems to have happened, so far as can be judged by the subsequent development of early social structures, is that whilst in some cases a sufficiently versatile and dominant leader would take it upon himself to be an oracle for truth as well as an oracle for action, in other cases, and these must have been the more numerous, some apparently gifted individual would be allowed to substantiate, or to have credited to him, a claim to special 'vision'. This vision was the happy faculty for discerning truth, and the nature and wishes of the gods in particular. The history of Israel affords examples of the leader-seer, like David, and of the co-operation, and later opposition, of temporal and prophetic authority. (David's period is perhaps not the best example, because prophetic and kingly functions were already separated, though the early kings retained a good deal of the priest-prophet in their make up. The Hebrew patriarchs are a truer example of undivided authority.) To the 'seers' was allowed power to declare 'This is what should be believed', or even, 'Thus saith the Lord'. It would be interesting to know what the relationships were, in the early societies, between these two types of authority, and to see whether both could be properly so called. As it is, we must suspect that just as the expression 'the authority of the facts' is metaphorical and the 'authority of the scientific expert' is metaphorical if it is used of his intra-scientific capacity as a truth-teller, so the authority of the original prophets, priests, or holy-men, was metaphorical. Its force, moreover, we would expect to have been derived from the ruler of the group because, just as all that was 'authoritative' had to derive its authority from him, so everything which was derived from him bore the stamp of his authority. We have seen how this process was worked out in later form in Egypt (p.3, *supra*), Persia, Babylon, and Israel (pp. 2ff., *supra*) in the closest possible relationship between the spiritual and the temporal authority, so that in many cases the spiritual function was assimilated to the temporal and the prestige of truth-telling was kept for the ruler. Even if spiritual knowledge or vision had been originally secondary, and derived authority from the concept of temporal leadership, as society developed in self-consciousness and religious practices developed in importance, the ruler could no longer simply sanction or concede religious authority. It had to be brought closer to his person, so that he could be seen to be the chosen of God or to stand in a special relationship with God, or to be himself of the quality of God. The last of these, of course, is the position to which Rome finally reverted.

 This or similar manœuvres to appropriate a form of power which became increasingly important as the civilizations of the ancient world developed, should not be allowed to obliterate the simple and presumably original relationship of authority which has tended to arise between men on the ground of some behavioural superiority or superiority of endowment possessed by one of them, or some of them. This kind of endowment has no relation to truth and therefore authority, if it is to this kind of relationship that it must be traced, was not originally concerned with truth. Its coerciveness is therefore misused if it is used to declare 'This is the nature of God', or 'That is how the world began', rather than, 'You must pay taxes and perform military service'. If this view of the origin of authority is substantially correct, the derived view of an authority for truth is metaphorical, or at least secondary.

It may be objected, of course, that the form of development suggested here is not supported by a great deal of evidence, that it depends upon our rather slender knowledge of the origin of society, part of that based upon the probable analogy offered by modern 'primitives' and by psychological data which can be presented in different ways for different purposes. A rival theory might therefore be advanced to suggest that secular and spiritual authorities were originally distinct and developed along parallel courses until circumstances led to some degree of identification or mutual encroachment. It seems likely, however, that the earliest stage of religious apprehension was a vague belief in some kind of all-pervading energy—a sense of the diffusion of life or spirit throughout nature—and that this stage did not begin with spiritual experts or visionaries. It is not possible to say at what stage there began to be a recognition of special 'spiritual' qualities in individuals, but it is clear that the progress of authority would be more rapid in matters less mysterious and on the basis of qualities less difficult to assess.

Looked at another way, the concept of a religious relationship with a power or powers seems to have developed on the analogy of human relationships—even in the highly developed cultures of the ancient world the gods were manlike and the functions they discharged were those of kings, warrior leaders, fathers, and physicians, governing their people, destroying their enemies, healing their diseases and making their animals and fields fruitful. We may surely assume that the human relationships on which the relationships of religion were analogized were prior to them. This again would suggest that the secular authority relationship comes before the sacred one.

Or if we view the matter from the standpoint of the development of the human psyche itself, it is reasonable to suppose that imaginative insights and speculations, however primitive, would not have developed as early as simple relationships based on the need for food and security.

If the general trend of these arguments is reliable there is some reason to believe that the idea of authority in religion has derived its imperative content from a secular relationship, and has added to that its own content of esoteric knowledge. The result of this sort of combination would be to associate the transmission of such knowledge with coercive power—to move from the primitive secular 'You must do this!' to the less fittingly peremptory 'This is true', or its more overtly authoritarian corollary: 'You must believe this.'

Even if this is true, it does not necessarily invalidate the method of authority in religion, though it may cause us to look twice at its claims. Even if authority in religion is a concept which was originally based on the secular leader-follower relationship, the subsequent development of authority in religion may have justified the original borrowing. It may be that what was at first merely an effective director of conduct, a device of rule, turned out to be suitable for the transmission of truth. That is a possibility which will be discussed when we consider how far authority is able to compel belief, or guarantee knowledge, or to disclose the truth.

*   *   *

Now let us consider the tasks which religious authority sets out to perform and the claims it makes upon us. First, it claims a certain regulative authority within a defined society. This is the authority of the Church which is needed to maintain its discipline and standards as a society. Second, there is the claim of a special relationship with truth, or with God in respect of truth, so that we ought to believe its deliverances. This claim is made sometimes on behalf of a Church or society, sometimes on behalf of a written communication, and sometimes it is claimed by an individual or of an individual.

Of the first claim of authority little need be said. Those who join a Church must be prepared to accept its traditional standards of discipline, behaviour, worship, and belief. Such a Church must obviously be conceded the right to say how its members shall conduct themselves in matters over which it claims jurisdiction, to declare what forms of worship and observance are acceptable to its tradition, and to indicate what has been its traditional standard of doctrine—to say what it believes officially, and what its members should believe. If this is merely an institutional arrangement one would have no fault to find with it from a philosophical point of view, though from a theological point of view there may be some cause for dissatisfaction with this as the ground-plan for a Church.

No intellectual impropriety would be committed if a body of people calling themselves 'The Church of the Baptist' should require that its members eat only locusts and wild honey, should be baptized in Jordan, and should believe in the divinity of John the Baptist. If would-be members of such a Church knew what was expected of them, it would not be a matter for complaint if they were subsequently excommunicated for failing to comply. The Roman Catholic who denies the doctrine of transubstantiation has no ground for complaint if he is excluded from the Roman communion. This internal authority must be conceded. A Church must have the right to say what it believes officially, and may insist upon conformity of belief, or even conformity of dress, as the Quakers did, or non-smoking, as the Salvation Army does. But this is not an authority which is peculiar to a Church as a Church. It is only the authority which may be claimed and exercised by a tennis club committee or a trades union.

The problem of authority in religion is not to be confounded with this question of institutional authority, though we may note in passing that it is fatally easy to pass over from the statement, 'This is what you must believe', to the statement: 'This is true.' It is to statements of the latter kind that we must now turn our attention, because this is where we begin to run into epistemological hazards.

In 1950 the Roman Church declared the dogma of the Assumption of the Blessed Virgin Mary to be *de fide*—and by that it should presumably be understood that this was not only something which Catholics ought henceforth to believe true, but something the truth of which was guaranteed by the declaration of the Church. The authority for this dogma is not to be found in scripture. A Catholic writer, at the time of the declaration, wrote: 'Scripture yields nothing that is directly relevant to our inquiry. . . . In the absence of clear scriptural evidence, it is to the second source of revealed truth, divine tradition, that theologians turn to discover our doctrine. . . . With this infallible definition, there is an end to any doubt the faithful may have had whether the Assumption is divinely revealed. . . . It is not for the individual Christian to declare what the *depositum fidei* contains, but only for the Church's Living Voice.'[6] By his definition, we assume that the Pope (using his title as a shorthand expression for the system of consultation which produced the definition) did not mean that what was previously untrue is now true; but what was formerly not guaranteed to be true is now so guaranteed. For the faithful only or for all men? The requirement of assent must be confined to the faithful, but the guarantee of truth surely cannot be restricted. We are dealing with a factual proposition: It is declared that Mary the mother of Jesus did not suffer physical death but was translated to Heaven. Now either she did die, in a physical sense which we all understand, or she did not. Some people in the past have believed that she did not die. No direct contemporary evidence can be appealed to—*The Tablet* statement concedes that—but a tradition to that effect had existed in the Church. Side by side with that tradition have existed other traditions, such as the tradition that certain of the saints can be of assistance to mundane mortals in such matters as finding lose articles or guiding lost travellers. But at the point of the Pope's definition the authority of the Church singled out a particular tradition and said, in effect: 'We now guarantee the truth of this.'

It might be objected that this is an overstatement of the case. Did the Pope mean only that Christians of the Roman obedience must now believe this to be true, but this is a matter of faith and not a matter of truth? Is it simply an invitation to faith and not a guarantee at all? Not so far as one can understand what the Roman Church teaches about the *ex-cathedra* pronouncements of the Pope. There is some clue to this in a paper read to the Oxford University Reunion Society in 1937 by Father Victor White, O.P. 'We would maintain that the Apostles were not only commissioned to teach and impose the revelation of Christ, but they were commissioned in such a way that in so doing they were infallible, and that such infallibility is a necessary corollary of their commission. In claiming infallibility for the apostles we do not mean that their words or even their ideas were immediately inspired; infallibility is not inspiration, still less is it verbal dictation or even divine assistance in the choice of words. Nor do we claim that, in virtue at any rate of their infallibility, any new revelation was made to

---

[6] G. D. Smith in *The Tablet* (28th October, 1950), quoted by J. K. S. Reid in *The Authority of Scripture* (Methuen, 1957), p. 136.

them, or that they were able to make oracular pronouncements as mediums of divinity. We mean simply that they were so assisted by God that they were rendered incapable of teaching error in exercising their apostolic function of teaching the revelation of Christ to the nations.'[7] This explanation is offered to show the context of papal infallibility which is thought to arise from an authority continuous with that of the Apostles and from the apostolic nature of the Pope's office. Canon Richards adds a comment of his own: 'The Church's inherent *infallibile magisterium* is limited to declaring what is the Catholic Faith and rejecting false teaching. It is not a device for answering all sorts of religious questions as if it were an easy method of arriving at the truth. It is strictly limited to the task of bearing a faithful and reliable witness to the Faith as received from Christ and his Apostles, and when need arises to determine its true implications.'[8]

It is still not clear what the status of an infallible pronouncement is intended to be. Is it true that the '*Magisterium* is limited to declaring what is the Catholic Faith'? We have conceded that an internal arrangement of this kind is permissible in any society, but that the granting of this kind of authority has nothing to do with the question of truth. The Christian Scientist is exercising his *magisterium* legitimately when he tells his fellow Christian Scientists that Mrs Eddy considered matter to be illusionary and unreal. He is still being faithful to his commission if he infers from that the heartening message that there is no such thing as a thermo-nuclear bomb. If he claimed infallible authority for this pronouncement we should not feel much need to dispute it. But neither would we abandon our lively and apprehensive belief in the reality of thermo-nuclear power. Is the Church of Rome only claiming that sort of infallibility? If so, it can be of interest only to members of that communion, or at the most, to other Christians who may be anxious lest the device of infallibility shall add any more novel items in such a way as to embarrass their own apologists.

Where does the question of truth enter into all this? In the case of the dogma of the Assumption, is the Church simply saying: 'We are now making the proclamation, not that the Virgin Mary

---

[7] Quoted by Canon Rich in his *Spiritual Authority in the Church of England* (Longmans, 1953), p. 212.
[8] ibid., pp. 212-13.

was translated to Heaven without physical death, but that this is what the Apostles taught, and in this we cannot err'? If so, the demonstration of the truth of the actual occurrence rests on the belief of the Apostles and all that is now guaranteed is another truth, 'This is what they believed and taught', and this is inerrant. Or is the Church saying: 'The Virgin Mary did not, in fact, die'? In neither case, it seems to us, can the conclusion be avoided that there is a guarantee of truth. If the guarantee is primarily attached to the facts about the end of the Virgin's earthly life, then it is a remarkable guarantee. If, on the other hand, it is simply a statement, 'It is true beyond doubt that the Apostles taught', it is less remarkable but still surprising. If this were the Christian Scientist we could easily understand his reference to Mrs Eddy's teaching to mean, 'There is a statement in a book believed to be by Mrs Eddy, to the effect that . . .'. But the statement of the Church could hardly be so simple as that. No plain apostolic authority seems to exist for it. This is something that came to be believed about Mary and was then attributed to the tradition handed down by the Apostles. Now, after nearly two thousand years, during which the Church has not been sure of this, or has not said so, it is now able to say, 'It is true that they taught this'.

This is not a criticism of the dogma, or of the Roman Church for defining the dogma. Such criticisms must be offered and answered, in the main, inside the discipline of theology. But we would appear to have established that on either of these interpretations of the nature of an infallible pronouncement of this sort, there is a claim of truth in a matter of fact. And for the fact or facts alleged what is offered is not, in the final resort, evidence (though evidence may be offered) but the guarantee of an infallible authority.

* * *

We turn now to a second appeal to authority in religion which again involves the notion of a special relationship with truth. The characteristic Christian form of this is the appeal to the authority of the Bible as an infallible source of truth. We have seen that in Protestantism there was a tendency from the beginning to exalt the authority of scripture in order, it is said, to supply the want of the ecclesiastical authority which was renounced with the renunciation of Rome. From the time of the Reformation the notion not simply of the authority of the Bible, but of its infallibility, has produced some strange forms of religious allegiance and practice. This has been especially true during the last century or so, partly as a reaction against the critical study of the Bible and, at the moment, there are millions of people who are committed to the belief that 'every word in the Bible is true'.

More modest claims have been made on behalf of the Bible and we shall consider some of them later. For the moment, however, we shall see our way better if we consider the extreme form in which biblical authority is maintained. The idea of word-for-word inspiration and inerrancy was taken over from the later Jewish attitude to the canon of the Old Testament and spread gradually to the Christian writings. But, as Reid points out the Christian Fathers allowed allegorical and highly fanciful interpretations to be practised, and you can cheerfully allow yourself to be tied to the words of any statement so long as you are, at the same time, allowed to attach your own meaning to it.[9] Modern literalists, however, have tried to get rid of allegorical interpretation and still to preserve the letter of the Bible. We do not need to examine the position to make sure whether there is a claim of authority for truth, as we did in the case of the Roman claim. There is no attempt to rationalize, as a rule. The claim is quite simply, as one has heard it expressed in public by a fundamentalist of patent sincerity: 'I believe every word in the Bible—simply because it is in the Bible. If I doubted one word, I might as well doubt it all.'

Again, the claim to reach truth and to proclaim truth by a method of authority is what interests us. This is not a rational attitude and does not pretend to be, so that to point out the obvious inconsistencies which are involved, and even the impiety of 'levelling' the content of the Bible by a doctrine which makes every word 'true', would probably be a waste of time. We will consider later some alternative theories about the truth of the Bible, but for the present it is sufficient to confront ourselves with the bare assertion that anyone who wishes to call himself a Christian must believe everything in the Bible because it is 'true'. Just as, in the first type of religious authority, the Apostles were considered to have been rendered incapable of error in their official capacity, so in this uncompromising view of the authority of

---

[9] *The Authority of Scripture*, p. 27.

Scripture the writers are claimed to have operated under an inspiration so total that what they wrote was wholly the word of God and contained nothing that was due to their own proneness to error.

The third type of religious authority which claims a special appropriation of truth is that which we associate with the inspired individual. His claim is to a special relationship with God which may be regarded as private, in which there is no overt claim to regulate the beliefs of others, or public, in which case the individual experience is regarded as normative. The claim to have enjoyed this kind of experience (if 'enjoyed' is the right word) goes back a long way in the history of religion. It was claimed by the Pythagoreans, at one extreme of religious experience, and by Socrates at the other. The great prophets of Israel represent a relatively exalted form of the tendency and their cry, 'Thus saith the Lord', has been listened to with a good deal of respect—the more so since they backed their claim to prophetic insight with an undeniable insight into the moral and political condition of their people. In the Christian Church this individualistic claim to religious authority is associated particularly with the period after the Reformation, not because there were no individuals with a claim of inspiration before that (though life was more difficult for them), but because after the Reformation the authority of individual experience was recognized to be a serious factor in the religious community.

From Luther onward we are made very much aware of the claim of personal experience to apprehend and to transmit truth. Those who followed Luther waited for the primary evidence of their mended relationships with God in a change of their own consciousness rather than in the guarantee of the Church. Calvin had stressed that before anyone could perceive even the truth of the Bible he must receive the gift of heightened spiritual perception from the Spirit of God. Following these traditions, and laying a little more emphasis on the subjective aspect, the Quakers found their supreme authority in the 'inner light'. So far as this meant that individual experience was the ultimate guide in religion, it pursued a method quite different from that of authority. In due course, however, this kind of thinking produced its own claims to individual infallibility and where this enlightened condition was conceived to be the prerogative of only some members of a religious community, those individuals assumed a characteristic 'charismatic' authority. Wesley, who laid a very considerable stress on the need for religion to be personally felt, was himself disturbed at the effect produced on his societies by the infiltration of the notion that individual inspiration is supreme. The folk who were affected by this idea tended to regard themselves as altogether above the law, divine or human, and as having no need for Bible, Church or sacraments. The milder and the more flagrant examples of this tendency were lumped together by more orthodox eighteenth-century churchmen and called 'enthusiasts'.

* * *

We must now look more carefully at the nature of these claims of authority. For the time being, we do not need to separate them, since it is with a general principle that we shall be concerned initially. The disputed territory is 'truth'. We have agreed that authority in religion is entirely competent for the purposes of discipline and organization: ethical questions about the employment and degree of authority may arise, but there is no epistemological problem. But in what sense can a religious authority claim to guarantee the truth of its deliverances? In what way does the statement, 'Christ died on the Cross' differ from 'The Bible (or the Church) says Christ died on the Cross'? This is surely a matter on which nobody's inspiration is of much use. It is a statement about an alleged occurrence in history—more obviously so in the first form. Either we have enough evidence for supposing that this took place or we have not. The authority of the Church may say to me, 'You ought to believe this', or even, 'You must believe this or cease to be a Christian', but what is the relationship which is supposed to make the pronouncement 'Christ died on the Cross', when declared by authority, the explicit guarantee for me that this occurrence actually took place. (We have chosen a plain historical statement for the purpose of discussion because it might be less easy to pin down the meaning of a statement like 'Jesus was the Son of God', though we should assume that, with due allowance for metaphor, this statement is meant to be true in the same sense as the first.) It does not seem sufficient to say, 'This is the apostolic witness': which in fact is to say, 'We guarantee that the Apostles believed and taught this, therefore it is true.' To say this is to provide a good reason for Christians to believe it, because

Christians must have the most careful regard for all that they can discover about the attitude of the Apostles to Jesus. This is proximate witness, but it is evidential—it carries no guarantee. Still we ask where the guarantee is supposed to come from, and what a guarantee for truth could possibly be.

In the case of biblical authority, Calvin taught that the 'authentification' of scripture was an activity of the Spirit of God which led men to discern its truth. But could that idea not have been used equally well to support the authority of the Church? If I say that this source of information is authoritative because I have discerned it to be so because of a personal revelation or enlightenment which was an activity of God, surely I am making the authority of Church and Bible dependent on my own 'prophetic' authority. Yet presumably at some stage in this train of witness someone is laying claim to a truth-guaranteeing state of mind. If there is no such state of mind, it will follow that this particular use of the word 'authority' in religion must be regarded as metaphorical.

It is notoriously difficult to prove so general a negative, but we may be able to form some reasonable opinions about this. It is generally agreed that when I say 'I know that my ink-bottle is now empty' my state of mind, expressed by that statement, is about the nearest I can get to an apprehension of truth. Leaving philosophical scepticism on one side, and assuming the normality of my perception and the rationality of my mind, this sort of knowing is about as sure as anything can be. It is clear, moreover, that if anyone does not share my experience of the ink-bottle, I cannot transmit my knowing to them. Our own knowing can have the immediacy and certainty which provide the greatest possible guarantee for us that something is the case. It is that immediacy and certainty which we seek to communicate whenever we add to the barest meaning of 'know' the notion of inerrancy which is implicit in, 'I don't think or imagine or suppose that the bottle is empty, I know it'. This one assumes to be as 'clear and distinct' as it is possible for knowledge to be, unless it be thought that certain *a priori* principles are as distinct. The question we have now to ask ourselves is: 'Can such immediacy of knowledge, which carries its own certificate of truth for those who experience it, be transferred to others? Can it ever carry the same guarantee for them? If I report to my next visitor that my ink-pot is empty and he later passes on the information to one of his friends, can he, in the mental transaction with his friend, be said to know about my ink-well's condition in the way that I could be said to know about it? We would think not. If he were challenged about the matter he might indeed say: 'But I *know* it is empty. He told me so himself.' This, however, would not be because I have been able to transfer my immediate knowledge, but because of an inference from what I have said and from his previous knowledge of me. Unless the experience of knowing which rests upon an original perceptive experience were somehow transferable or shareable (other than by sharing the original experience) in a way it apparently is not, it is difficult to see how a guarantee of truth can be passed from one person to another. Something fairly near to a guarantee can be transferred, but we call this evidence and it establishes every degree of likelihood short of certainty.

In matters of simple experience we tend to regard the sort of evidence we have come to accept as appropriate in particular sets of circumstances as 'practically' certain, but the amount and kind of evidence we require depends upon the simplicity or complexity of events to which we are asked to give credence, as well as such circumstances as their remoteness in time or their remoteness from common experience. If our neighbour were to report that his dog had been missing all day, we should probably require nothing more than his statement to convince us. If, however, he were to report that his wife had fallen downstairs, we might possibly have a flicker of doubt about 'fallen'. And even the assurance, 'She fell by herself', would not in itself enable us to feel that we had a sure state of knowledge about the truth of what happened, as we had in the case of the dog. Now the statements which are made to us by religious authorities are generally about matters which are still more remote from our first-hand knowledge. If it is the business of authority in religion, with regard to truth, simply to present us with overwhelming evidence, that would be perfectly acceptable and would at least enable us to claim some degree of assurance about the well-foundedness of our beliefs. But surely the three types of authority we have discussed, infallible book, infallible Church, and inspired individual, do not merely claim to lay evidence before us? Perhaps we should understand that they are claiming to replace the function of the ink-bottle itself. A deliverance of a religious authority might be thought to resemble the presented bottle, the thing in itself, or so far as it is responsible for my sensations; the actuality, whatever it is, which leaves me in no doubt at all that I am in need of ink. Similarly, it might be argued, you can see the Church, you can encounter its faith and its worship as present actualities, and you can encounter the message of the Bible similarly, with the same actuality that you can encounter an ink-bottle, and then you must leave the Bible and the Church to be their own expositors and to supply their own overtones. This does in fact indicate one way in which both Bible and Church have been presented.

If this were adequate, an encounter with Church or Bible or inspired individual would leave little more to be desired. Such experience would enable us to attain a direct apprehension of religious truth, and to know it with the certainty with which we know the ink-bottle. But the matter to be known is not simple, and what is to be apprehended is not the content of a sense-experience. At the best, this only indicates how a religious authority could possibly be perceived, as it were, in the place of the less easily perceived truth which is the more remote object of our faith. But because this can be done, it does not follow that the almost compulsive knowledge of the ink-bottle variety can be obtained of spiritual truths—or not by this method. If we sought a perceptual knowledge of the same kind, all we would arrive at would be a completely convincing experience of a book with leaves of paper and a leather cover, or a building, or a man in ecclesiastical apparel, or a painting, or the sum of such experiences. But our problem is to go behind these to their religious implications. It is as though we were warned that what really mattered about the ink-bottle was the unhappy married life of the man who screwed on the cap before it left the factory. Or even, more credible and proximate, that the ink in the bottle, now only a smear on the bottom, was made from a derivative of coal. We should have little difficulty in accepting that, but we could hardly be said to know it in the sense of having an immediate awareness, as we are aware of the existence of the bottle. Nor is it easy to see how either a Church or a book could give us that kind of knowledge of matters which they *are* not themselves but which they only report or present.

It is easy to see why, in this connexion, so much reliance has been placed on the third type of authority, the authority of individual vision. Here we have what appears to be a good analogy with perceptive knowledge. If it is true that the prophetic or spiritually perceptive person perceives religious truths in the direct way in which ordinary individuals perceive ink-bottles, then we can understand why they feel certain that they have experienced something which is real, and which is as true for others as themselves, just as the ink-bottle is. But are we right to call this an authority, in respect of truth, for others? The compulsiveness, the certainty of knowing, is necessarily first-hand and it is intransmissible, so far as we know, unless we can contrive to duplicate or represent the original experience. Generally we have to be content to recreate our experience for others by description and explication. This seems to be all that the prophet can do, and yet it omits precisely that directness of apprehension which appears to be the only thing which can compel our belief. We have not been able to find a truth-guaranteeing state of mind except the immediate awareness we have in sense experience, or possibly in the apprehension of a necessary truth such as the principle of contradiction. Our state of certainty is not, in any case, a guarantee in the same sense for others. It is not transmissible. Anything short of such a guarantee is evidence, and we must conclude that this is what the Bible and the Church and the inspired individual have to offer.

If all this is true, how is it that claims to be or to provide authority for truth have been made so widely and admitted to frequently? This is not mere human folly, for some of the most intelligent and perceptive people still contribute to the recognition of such authorities. We believe that the answer is to be found in the development of the concept of authority. If, as we have already suggested, a simple imperatival relationship was the original form of authority—a relationship based upon some kind of pre-eminence in an individual, then the deliverances of such an authority would take the form of commands or prohibitions. Even in the comparatively advanced civilizations of the ancient world intellectualization of religion was a fairly late development. We should expect to find, certainly in the earlier stages of religion, that religious injunctions were not passed on as apprehensions of truth to be considered as evidence for belief, but as simple commands to worship and to propitiate the usual Gods in the usual manner. Hence the idea of a traditional 'authority' for religious matters would not have been strange in any society where observances and customary behaviour were generally subject to regulation.

Somewhere along the line, however, someone has gone a little farther and has made his sacred inscriptions, or his regulations about sacrifice, or his own religious consciousness not only regulative for the behaviour of his fellows—which the law of conformity in the tribe would approve—but for their belief also. The step from 'You must *do* this', to 'You must *believe* this' is, as has already been indicated, only a small one. This process is all the easier to understand if we forbear from reading back into the past sophisticated notions about truth and knowledge and belief. Belief has sometimes been regarded, even in comparatively recent times, as a voluntary thing, and therefore an activity or attitude which could be regarded as praiseworthy or blameworthy. In earlier times there can have been little hesitation about telling a member of the community that he had to assent to the accepted beliefs about the gods, or else face penalties. Of course to assent to beliefs is not to believe, but the difference would hardly have worried even the majority of the Greeks of the generation of Socrates, far less their tribal ancestors. It was enough for the Western Catholic Church at the time of the Inquisition if would-be victims were willing to assent to the official dogmas. Belief viewed thus naïvely, as assent, is a form of behaviour which is to some extent regulable, and regulable by authority in the same way that sitting on the appropriate chair is regulable. We suggest some such basis for the view that has been held so widely that there can be an authority for truth which is able to say not merely, 'Here is what you ought to believe', but 'This is true because we say so'.

Before we go any farther we should perhaps look again at the efforts which have been made to present religious authority in a modified form which would meet some of the difficulties raised by our changing views about the Church and the Bible. To what extent can these be regarded as successful? Oman's 'authority' is found first in individual vision, which, as an insight into spiritual truth, conveys the kind of certainty which perception does in our relations with the physical world. This individual vision is then correlated with that of the religious community. There is no coercion of the individual, no pressure 'to receive anything on the assertion of another'.[10] Oman argues that we must see for ourselves, though we must check our vision against that of the visionary society—the Church. All this is excellent, but it is an account of an evidential method, not a method of authority in the strict sense. This distinction, at least, must be clear, or we shall never know when we are discussing authority and when we are not. Oman is looking for the ground of belief and he directs us to find it in an individual examination of the data. Authority which thus 'rests on freedom and individual vision realized and shared in the society of the Church' (p. 73 *supra*) is really not authority at all, it is the method of examining what facts there are and then consulting the comparable experience of others.

Forsyth was well aware of the need for a more objective concept of authority and he identified the authority-giving source as a series of acts of God in history which provide the original data for Christian faith. The authority here belongs to the original revelation and not to a book or a Church which have sprung from it as secondary sources. This revelation he calls 'the Christian Gospel' and he describes it as 'an authority for the will —in the will's sphere of history'. This is 'an authority which is felt primarily as living, moral majesty, not as truth'.[11] This comes much nearer to meeting the full requirements for an authority in religion. Forsyth pointed us to the Christian Gospel as a historic event and proclamation, and in this respect we may think that he was, like Oman, founding religion on evidence rather than on authority, but he then added the suggestion that the data of the Gospel were to act as directors of the will rather than as a communication of truth. Two points call for comment. First, it is not clear how we are to distinguish the original historical revelation from the account of it in book and tradition, when these are the only sources we have (apart from an examination of the consequences of the historical events, and of faith in them, upon subsequent history). At the time Forsyth wrote, there was still a good deal of optimism about the ability of scholarship, given time, to penetrate the infirmities and insights of the Bible and tradition and thus disclose the pristine revelation. The limitations of critical scholarship are now more generally realized. We can never know exactly what the events and proclamation were apart from the accounts we have of them, and we can only

[10] Oman, p. 182. [11] Forsyth, *The Principle of Authority*, p. 400.

recognize to a limited extent how the media of transmission may have obscured what they were intended to reveal. This should not matter unless we are trying to suggest that by 'authoritative', when applied to the deliverances of Bible and tradition, we imply 'literally inerrant'. This has been part of the meaning, so far as one can see, in biblical literalism and in claims of ecclesiastical infallibility. May not an account which contains some inaccuracy and some error still possess authority for us?

If we insist on looking for an authority for truth, the discovery and admission of a single error would be an embarrassment, though not necessarily a fatal one, unless we had come to regard our source as a mechanical oracular device. On the other hand, can one regard a book or a tradition which is incapable, rightly interpreted, of conveying information which is untrue in any respect, as anything but oracular, and would not a mechanical use of such an oracle be excusable? An authority for truth, even if we accept this difficult term for the moment, would only have to be true. But to say it was such an authority would be to say it was true—and so on. The only way to defend such a view is to argue that the book is true for some reason that is not, so to speak, proper or intrinsic to itself. It could be argued that the book was true because you guaranteed it (which is Rome's way out of the problem). Protestants who wish to find a guarantee of biblical authority seem to prefer to rely on the notion of the self-authentification of the Bible. The former device leaves the real authority with a hierarchy of men who guarantee the book and the tradition which guarantee them, while the latter does its utmost to leave authority within the covers of a self-authenticating book. Both these claims of authority are based upon circular reasoning, but it should be recorded that theologians sometimes admit as much without undue dismay.

If we were right in suggesting that the proper sphere of authority is not the determination of truth, so that the concept of an authority for truth is likely to lead us into difficulties, it may be the case that the existence of elements in either a book or tradition which cannot be known to be true may be of slight importance—or even totally irrelevant. Our discussion of the nature of authority at that point led us to recognize an 'imperatival' concept as probably the primary one from which later ideas of authority had developed. Forsyth seems to have found grounds for believing, from a theological point of view, that the primary authority in religion is of this kind: 'The Christian Gospel is an authority for the will in the will's sphere of history'.

Can we conceive of an authority for the will which need not be inerrant in all its statements of fact? This is an all too familiar pattern of human behaviour. At its least estimable, it is the ignorant sergeant-major issuing orders; at a higher level it is the uncertain schoolmaster running short of history and relying on the weight of his own personality. But at a much higher level, it is the moral imperative of the saintly life, an imperative whose force may be only a little impaired, or not at all, by the fact that the saint cherishes some ideas about science or economics, or even some ideas about religion, which fail to command our assent, or are even palpably untrue. We may feel that we must endeavour to emulate his saintliness without feeling any obligation to believe that everything he says is true. It will be enough, for the moment, if we envisage the possibility of such an authority. Later, we shall have to consider to what extent such a concept of authority is legitimate and satisfactory in the sphere of religion (see Chapter Seven).

Martineau's account of religious authority is based on his concept of the nature of the regulating authority in ethics. So far as our moral conduct is concerned, he believed that the regulative force was an intuitive one, and that the intuitive moral perception which we call conscience enables us to discern a revelation of the nature of God (it is a moral revelation) in Jesus Christ. Such an apprehension might be enough to enable us to identify a divine element in the story of Jesus, but it could say nothing very definite about the major dogmatic claims of the Christian faith. We are not simply invited to believe that in Jesus we are, as Martineau says, ushered into the presence of a real righteousness which indicates the nature of God to us—though that would not be a slight thing. We are invited to believe that Jesus was uniquely the Son of God and yet a veritable man, that his death was in some way sacrificially connected with human sin, that he rose from the dead, and that he lives still, not only in that spiritual remoteness which we call Heaven, but in the life of the Christian Church. This is a minimal account of what the Church invites men to believe, but the statement as we have presented it goes far beyond the range of the kind of authority suggested by Martineau. He would have agreed that this is so, for his own conviction was that rational matters must be decided by reason and moral matters by conscience. No amount of moral perceptiveness will enable us to come to the conclusion that Jesus rose from the dead, so that as far as Martineau is concerned, this would be a matter to be judged by reason—by consulting the evidence. He accepted this method and the limitations of the reduced form of Christian belief to which it led him.

Can we, in any case, be justified in calling a moral sense an authority? Perhaps Martineau is not technically guilty of this, for he envisages a moral universe, an objective 'good' in the Platonic sense;[12] but our only apprehension of this is what emerges in consciousness. If we are only able to say that something emerges in my consciousness which tells me that it is right to act in a particular manner, are we really speaking about a relationship of authority or simply using the word 'authority' in a much diluted metaphorical sense? In the end, Martineau goes beyond this subjectivism and points to an objective religious authority in what he calls 'the religion of Jesus'. Two comments seem to be called for. First, his 'religion of Jesus' is itself subjectively conceived. It is reached by a process of stripping away mythological accretions, and the stripping down process itself is regulated by certain principles of criticism which Martineau enunciates (ibid., pp. 54–6). This may be the right thing to do, but it is a curious way to come upon authority. One cannot but conclude that after we have finished our careful labour of reduction and elimination, in the Martineau manner, the authority that is left behind belongs to ourselves rather than to the postcritical precipitate.

The second comment concerns the moral nature of the authority which Martineau conceived to be basic for Christianity. Having reached his normative concept, 'the religion of Jesus', he recognizes in this relationship (between Jesus and God) not a dogma to convince, but a supreme good to compel moral agreement (see ibid., p. 610). This seems to bring us to a conclusion which has something in common with that of Forsyth. First we have a process which attempts to take us behind scripture and tradition to the events, or to a relationship revealed by the events, which produced them. Then we are pointed to an authority which

---

[12] Martineau, *The Seat of Authority in Religion*, p. 68.

Forsyth declares to be for the will and which Martineau regards as a moral imperative and one therefore which we presume could be thought of as to some extent, if not wholly, concerned with the will.

None of these attempts seem to have indicated a satisfactory 'truth guaranteeing' authority, yet we found this to be the real goal of the search for authority in religion.

It may be appropriate, at this point, to consider a little more closely what Karl Barth has had to say about one or two of the matters discussed by Oman, Forsyth, and Martineau. In a work of this kind an adequate exposition of Barthian theology cannot be undertaken, and could not even if we felt competent for the task, and it may be unfair to extract items and to consider these outside his theology as a whole: unfair, that is, from Barth's point of view, for he maintains that theological matters must always be theologically approached. So-called 'natural theology', which endeavours to reason from the nature and existence of the world to the nature and existence of its Creator, was totally repudiated by Barth, and this repudiation became one of the corner-stones of his theology: or perhaps it would be fairer to say that the reverse side of this repudiation of natural theology, Barth's entire reliance upon revelation, is the corner-stone. This revelation, which is for him the proper subject matter of all theological discourse, is the 'Word of God'. It would appear that we are presented with the idea of a theological circle, outside which we must not go in our quest for theological truth.

Barth's attitude to the authority of the Bible has had a tremendous effect on modern Protestantism. Many puzzled Christians had found themselves torn between the extremes of the ultra-conservative views of the literalists, on one hand, and the apparently ruthless biblioclasm of the left-wing critics, on the other. Barthianism has provided for them a synthesis which combines conservatism with criticism and adds, for good measure, a quite remarkable synthesis of holy mystery and intellectual agility. Barth would not be entirely patient with Forsyth's distinction between the biblical record and the 'act of Gospel' which Forsyth sees as a historical act of God lying behind the record of scripture. For Barth 'The relevant historical questions must be asked of the biblical texts, which in their very essence are witnesses'. The goal of biblical scholarship should be a unitary exegesis of the whole of the canonical scriptures as such, leaving aside 'the absurd purpose of trying to recover an historical truth lying behind the texts. The historical truth, which biblical science has to ascertain in its own way, lies in the meaning and continuity of the biblical texts themselves. Thus it is not distinct from the biblical truth which has to be sought'. 'Biblical truths must be investigated *for their own sake* because the revelation to which they bear witness stands, takes place, and is to be sought, not behind or above them, but in them.'[13]

One or two comments must be offered. First, there is the question of the 'theological circle'. It is not Barth alone who has reintroduced the notion that theological truth can only be reached by theological means, but since this notion is apparently fundamental to his theology we should consider how it affects the authority to which he points us. We have been able to see how a teaching authority may be created within a closed community and have concluded that there is no problem of validity so long as the authority makes statements such as: 'We believe in the therapeutic power of running water'. All this statement implies, so far as it is authoritative, is that such a belief is held within a particular community. If all such statements are gathered together, in the case of a single religious community, they will form an 'authoritative' credo. It is fairly plain to see that no claim of truth can be made for such statements outside the community in question, and certainly not on the ground that they are authoritative. On the other hand, it is difficult to believe, as we pointed out when we discussed the dogma of the Assumption of the Virgin Mary, that statements of this kind do not purport to state what is true, and true for all men. So it is easy for the valid authority which states and defines belief to evolve into an authority which is no longer valid, and which claims the right not only to declare, 'We believe that running water has therapeutic properties', but to add: '... and this is true, and can be known to be true by the fact of our declaration'.

If Barth wishes to say that the authority of the 'Word of God' is within the theological circle and that it conveys a truth which has no currency outside the circle, then this is a way of securing authority. But, as we have seen, the resultant authority is didactic

---

[13] Barth, *Kirchliche Dogmatik*, I.2.547-8; quoted from Hermann Diem, *Dogmatics* (Oliver and Boyd, 1959), pp. 60-1.

and says no more than: 'It is the case that such things as these are believed to be true by Christians'. It is a valid authority for definition but it isolates what it conveys from the criteria of truth which lie outside the circle. If the Christian Church wishes to continue to lay her doctrines before the world, she cannot seriously believe that they can be presented in such a way as to be, in principle, out of relationship with the general system of non-theological knowledge, and yet still command the respect and attention of those whose daily concern is with such knowledge. We wonder if the warning of Coleridge is apposite here: 'He who begins by loving Christianity better than the truth, will proceed by loving his own sect or church better than Christianity, and will end by loving himself better than all.'[14]

Our other comment on Barth concerns the attempt he has made to present to Christian faith an objective authority in the 'Word of God'. It is not the easiest thing in the world to discover what he means by the Word of God. According to the *Kirchliche Dogmatik* the Word of God takes a threefold form as the preached word, the written word, and the revealed word. The revealed word, which is presumably the primary source of authority, is known only from the scripture as adopted by the Church's proclamation—which is itself based upon scripture. 'We know God's written word only by the revelation which releases the proclamation or by the proclamation which is realized by revelation. We know the preached word only as we know the revelation attested by scripture or as we know the scripture which bears witness to revelation' (I.124). We presume this is saying, in a somewhat gothic manner, what the Word of God is to be distinguished as some sort of reciprocation between the actual words of scripture and the proclamation of Christian dogma by the Church. Having secured this tenuous concept of the Word of God, Barth goes on to say that 'the possibility of a knowledge of God's word lies in God's word and nowhere else' (I.234), and that our faith is solely due to the action of God's word. The Word overcomes our inability to receive revelation from God and restores our capacity for God.

It seems clear, at least, that the final authority appealed to is the whole content of scripture, but scripture interpreted as a whole by the living response of the Church. If we are still expecting to

---

[14] Quoted by A. L. Drummond, *German Protestantism Since Luther* (Epworth Press, 1951), p. 138.

find here an authority for truth of the sort we have criticized, another infallible truth-teller, we shall be disappointed. Barth does not indicate such an authority. Whatever truth-telling authority we choose, our confidence in it is liable to be shaken when we realize that we ourselves have done the choosing, so that it may owe its authority, to some extent, to our nomination. What Barth was trying to make clear was that the authority he had responded to was one that had chosen him. If his definitions do not always seem too clear to us it may be, save for our stupidity, because he was not the definer but the respondent. There emerges the possibility that such an authority may not have been conceived as an authority for the intellect, or if it was so conceived, it has turned out to be something else. Drummond comments (*German Protestantism Since Luther*, p. 167) that 'Lack of logical, psychological and sociological relevance has not prevented Barthianism from making strong appeal to the will and imagination'. This suggestion has a bearing upon our speculation concerning the original nature of the authority relationship. It may be possible to develop it a little farther in the course of our consideration of the legitimate uses of the method of authority in religion.

There is one more use of the term 'authority' in religious discussion which should be mentioned, if only for the sake of completeness. There is an illustration of its use in Drummond's *German Protestantism*. A footnote (op. cit., p. 140) refers to the statement of a German 'modernist' society of the 1860's—the '*Protestantenverein*', that 'The higher reason only has unconditional authority, and the Bible must justify itself before its tribunal'. We are not really concerned to know whether this is a good theological principle, but whether it is a proper use of the word 'authority' in a religious context. Quite simply, the statement implies that we think about the Bible and that there is an authority for truth involved, which is not to be found in what we attend to, but in the act of thinking. This is understandable if it means that the Bible must make sense to us or it cannot obtain our consent or acquiescence. If the Bible says that the insanity of the man among the tombs was caused by demon-possession and that the demons were transferred by Jesus to some nearby pigs, the story and its implications will have to submit to some rational examination before I can accept it as meaningful for me. It may be that my contribution would be the initial conviction that insanity is not caused by evil spirits and that it is frequently cured or alleviated without appeal to the notion of possession. Moreover, since the mental condition of the man was proper to his own psycho-physical constitution it could not be transferred to pigs any more than a fault in an aeroplane engine could be conveniently transferred to an adjacent railway engine. Very soon we have acquired an amended form of the story. A man apparently suffered from a psychosis and was allegedly cured by Jesus, and a disturbance took place among some pigs who were in the vicinity. This is a perfectly understandable way of treating such a story, though most modern exegetes would tend to approach the story more sympathetically and be more concerned to discover what the New Testament is trying to convey by the story. It is not, however, an instance of the use of authority, as the statement of the *Protestantenverein* would have us believe. We have sought agreement for the assertion that the true relationship of authority is one of effective command and compliance. To substitute for this effective command, which comes to us from outside (however it may come through the mechanisms of our sensation and understanding), our own internal dialectic which may precede obedience if the externally imposed imperative is not completely efficient and is in conflict with our own knowledge or our self-regard, is not to appeal to authority. It is to appeal away from authority. It would be better, therefore, if we were to avoid altogether such imprecise expressions as 'the authority of reason'.

CHAPTER SEVEN

THE LEGITIMACY AND LIMITATIONS OF THE METHOD OF AUTHORITY IN RELIGION

IN THE course of the previous chapter we were able to reach some tentative conclusions, first about authority generally and then about the use of the concept of authority in religion. Our inquiry into the nature of the authority relationship itself seemed to indicate that in its original sense authority consisted in the power or ability to direct or regulate the behaviour of others. When, however, we turned our attention to the manifestations of authority in religion, we found that although there was still a claim to regulate behaviour, there was also a claim to transmit truth. We concluded that if this simply meant that the deliverances of a religious authority were true in the sense that they were faithfully conveyed tradition ('This is an authoritative statement of what Christians have always believed'), such a claim might be understood as a proper function of the internal regulative authority of a community founded upon certain beliefs or tenets.

It appeared to be the case, however, that religious authority often claimed much more than this authority to define. It has claimed and claims the right to make declarations upon authority which are intended to be true absolutely, and which are to be known as true because they are so declared by authority. This seemed to involve the need for someone to enjoy what we called a truth-guaranteeing state of mind. We could find no justification for the belief that such a state of mind ever exists; except perhaps in the act of simple perception, where we presumably accept a state of mind as the guarantee of certain 'facts' about the world. This immediate experience does carry, for ourselves, a guarantee of actuality (even though in some cases we may have to admit that the nature of an experience has been misconstrued), but such a 'guarantee' is not transmissible. It cannot be offered to others as a state of mind, or an experience, but only as a statement about a state of mind which we have enjoyed. In short, our states of mind can only be offered as evidence, and they cannot afford to others a direct perception of what is the case. But if we can only offer evidence for truth we cannot offer authority for truth, unless we agree to give authority such a reduced meaning. We have seen that this reduced meaning is common, so that when we accept 'on authority' statements from persons who appear to be properly qualified to make them, this only means that we accept their statements as more or less reliable evidence. I may accept, upon the authority of my doctor, the assurance that I am suffering from an incurable disease, but the matter does not end there. I may go to the length of saying 'I know that I am suffering from Brown's syndrome, and that it is incurable', and add: 'I know because my doctor says so'. But this is evidently just a matter of persuasive evidence and not of knowledge. If, a week after the doctor's disclosure, I am introduced to a physician who is known to be a specialist in the diagnosis and treatment of Brownianism, and he tells me it is quite certain that I have never had such a disease, I will now go to my friends and tell them, with due relief, that I am not suffering from the syndrome, and that I know this to be so because the consultant told me so.

We may be able to see the admissibility in religion of this kind of authority which can only be called 'authority for truth' if we understand that we are not using 'authority' with its original force. We must see, too, that such authority can only present truth for acceptance and offer the additional weight of commendation represented by its own status as specialist. The authority for truth in such a case would be evidence—not the *prima facie* evidence contained in the nature of the fact or truth to be presented, but the kind of evidence which depends on the nature of the source of information. This train of thought may be made clearer if we consider an example. The statement 'Christ rose from the dead' would be one for which, if our suppositions about the nature of religious authority are true, we could not expect to find any guarantee in a state of someone else's mind or in a document reporting such a state of mind. We could however, receive the story from the Gospels or from the traditions of the Church, not as necessarily true, but as supported by the kind of evidence which we are calling authority. Such authority has degrees of evidential value, so that we can speak of 'good' or 'bad' authority, but so long as it is evidential it can never be absolute authority, for absolute authority is the quality of a command which cannot be resisted, not of a guarantee which cannot be mistaken.

It should be possible now to designate the forms of authority which we have come to regard as valid in religion. First, there is the regulative authority which we must concede to a system or community. This includes the right to define the doctrinal basis on which the system or community rests and to determine what are the conditions which would-be members must fulfil. The authority so claimed and conveyed is intra-mural.

Second, there is the evidential authority referred to in the last paragraph but one. This is a metaphorical use of the word 'authority' and it would be better called 'witness' or 'testimony'. (The Apostles themselves, whom the Church generally regards as the primary 'authorities' for the truth of the facts upon which the Christian Faith was based, were themselves called witnesses [Acts 1^{22}; 2^{32}; 3^{15}; 5^{32}, etc.]).

Is it possible to go further than this? Not, one would think, with such solid ground beneath our feet. These two authorities are limited but we can be perfectly sure that they are serviceable and we need not feel guilty of inconsistency or irrationality if we treat them with the respect which we discover to be due to them. But 'to treat with respect' or 'to consult' are not expressions which indicate the kind of response one would make to an authority which was authoritative in what we considered to be the primary sense. Surely the relationship should be expressed on the side of authority by words like 'direct' or 'command', and on our side by words like 'obey' or 'submit'? Yet we have seen that such expressions are not appropriate to the process of acquiring knowledge (though they could be—unideally perhaps—to the regulative authority of a Church). Is it possible that when religion has felt that it has discovered an authority for the intellect or for knowledge, it has really been discovering an authority for the will? We noticed some suggestions to this effect in Martineau and Forsyth. The authority to which Martineau directed us was one which he saw as decisive for moral action rather than for truth (p. 79, *supra*) while Forsyth speaks of the Christian Gospel as 'an authority for the will in the will's sphere of history' (p. 76, *supra*). We may also recall Drummond's comment on the effect of the Barthian search for authority, that it makes a 'strong appeal to the will and imagination' (p. 125, *supra*). If it were indeed possible to have an authority for the will in religion as distinct from an authority for the intellect, and if it could be effective as a basis of individual faith, and if such an authority were discernible apart from simple disciplinary authority, and resided in some fundamental aspect of the Christian Faith, as Forsyth suggested, then we should have to go no further to find a concept of authority at once adequate for religious need and closely akin to the most primitive and imperatival form of authority.

There is, however, a question which must be asked about the possibility of such an authority. Is it possible to by-pass the process of intellectual criticism and act by authority upon the individual will? Unhappily, we have seen this process at work too often to have any doubt about its feasibility. The degree of intellection which is interposed between stimulus and response is widely variable and we recognize that the circuit of response can be shortened so as to exclude, to all intents and purposes, critical reflection. Broadly speaking, this is the process of conditioning and its part in the development of an authority relationship is not difficult to see. By this process a dependable response to authority may be built up gradually until the operative factors are almost wholly confined to the authority symbols and the response. There is an increasingly automatic response which is not affected as much as it might be by the nature of the deliverances of the authority. Thus the convert to an authoritarian religious system may have to preface his submission by a good deal of hard thinking—more or less, depending on the state of his own inclinations. But when he has made his submission he feels that a great weight has been lifted from his mind. Henceforth individual decisions relating to the content of faith can be left to the Church. Meanwhile however, accustomed reliance upon authority increases for us the effectiveness of its injunctions and makes our response not only more sure, but dependable over a wider range of subject matter. It is at this stage that we are apt to accept without prior criticism, or in spite of criticism, declarations upon authority, the content of which we should previously have regarded as intellectually suspect.

If this is a substantially true account of the way in which we may become conditioned to respond to authority, there is good reason for accepting the idea that it is possible to have 'an authority for the will'. This need not be regarded as a precise expression. From the psychological point of view the response may be more complex than the expression suggests, but it may be allowed to stand as broadly descriptive of one phase or aspect of authority as we actually encounter it. It is clear how greatly a peremptory authority of this sort differs from one which directs by means of a presentation to our intelligence. One is an authority which we feel we *must* obey and the other an authority which we merely consult. The latter we called an 'authority for truth' and we see now why it is essential that it should always be distinguished from what we have called, tentatively, 'an authority for the will'.

To return to the suggestions of Martineau and Forsyth: In what sense could we regard a religious proclamation or a religious body or dignitary as an authority for the will? Could such an authority supply the need, which religious people have evidently felt, for an authority for truth? Perhaps the answer may be forthcoming if we pose a further question: What does an authority for the will accomplish? If we re-examine the relationship of master and boy in the acts of command and obedience when a schoolmaster says, 'Sit down', we shall find that although these interpersonal relationships are never so simple as they seem, the ingredient which predominates is simple obedience. Within a fairly wide range of possible activities the schoolmaster with a well-developed authority can induce his pupils, or most of them, to act with very little reflection or none at all. This authority is exerted in order to maintain a disciplined relationship. There is an element of respect for superiority in the boys' side of the relationship, either intellectual or physical superiority, or both, but it also rests upon the prerogative of office. The proper function of such authority is to control the behaviour of children, but in practice it does a good deal more than that. There must be very few parents who have not found in their children, from time to time, the most curious beliefs. One child suddenly decides that all meat is poison, another that beer is an excellent antiseptic, another that the night air is injurious to health. Upon closer examination, it becomes evident that these are some of the idiosyncratic beliefs of masters and mistresses which have been passed on to children under the seal of authority. It is not, one would think, that authority has been deliberately used for this purpose, but that the random statements of an established authority still carry some of its compulsive force. An authority for the will, then, is likely to fulfil not only its primary purpose, which is to regulate behaviour, but secondary purposes; or to achieve unpurposed effects. It may be an effective means of inducing belief. The beliefs which are so induced are not necessarily true beliefs, or even likely to be true, since they may have nothing to do with the reason for the establishment of the authority.

This is all commonplace if we think only of the relationship of a schoolmaster with his pupils, but it may not be quite so easy to discern what limits should be set to the function of such an authority in a religious setting. Leaving aside the schoolmasterly or disciplinary authority of the Church, which raises no problems so long as it confines itself to discipline, we have already examined and criticized the notion of an authority for truth, and the suggestion has been entertained that an authority for the will might conceivably replace an authority for truth so far as religion is concerned. If, when Forsyth claimed that the Gospel was an authority for the will, he meant that the example of the life and death of Jesus inclines us to act in certain ways, this is a mere truism. But the claim seems to be that the Gospel inclines us to believe, not by an 'authoritative' declaration of truth, the possibility of which we have been led to doubt, but by an effective suasion of the will. 'It (the Christian Gospel) is not for the intellect —except so far as the intellect depends on the will. It is an authority which is felt primarily as living moral majesty, not as truth— as Christ was felt, not as the Scribes.'[1]

We have granted that disciplinary authority can achieve, sooner or later, a virtual exemption from intellectual scrutiny, and can incline us to act for no reason except that we are so instructed. It does not need any stretch of the imagination to see that the process which works in the schoolroom could work in the Church. That the pupils will not all be young and impressionable would not matter, since effective training during the formative years will, in most cases, ensure continued compliance, and most adults in the Church have been trained in it as children. There seems to be no reason why a similar attitude should not be built up toward the injunctions and significant events communicated by a sacred literature. We might allow then that both the characteristically Catholic authority of the Church and the Protestant authority of scripture might act as authorities for the will, directing conduct by a process that makes slight reference to the intelligence.

---

[1] Forsyth, *The Principle of Authority*, p. 400.

And when that has been admitted, it is difficult to resist the conclusion that such authority might be used effectively to induce belief. But we saw that beliefs which are passed to children under the suasion of disciplinary authority are to be regarded as illegitimately conveyed (though the process in that case is unavoidable and is only tolerable because of the good faith of teachers generally and the limited opportunity of re-forming beliefs at a later stage of development), and we see no reason to doubt that to induce belief in religion by a device which operates in the same manner is equally illegitimate. This seems to be a mode of the fallacy of misplaced authority. What is conceded to a disciplinary ecclesiastical authority is the right to define the teachings of the ecclesiastical body in question and to govern the conduct of its members in those matters which affect their standing as members. If this power were used deliberately to change belief, or to mould belief, to induce beliefs which might or might not be true, then it would surely be an improper use of authority. Yet this is done, and done widely in any system of belief which is enshrined in its own ethos and surrounded by its own mystique. Religious educators remind us that Christianity is caught rather than taught. After all, it could be objected, the authority in question is only promulgating the beliefs which are the agreed foundation of the sort of faith a member of that Church should possess. It might be argued, 'Supposing that you are brought up in our system and accept our beliefs on authority, not after critical examination, but because you have learnt to respect and obey the officers and institutions of our authority since you were a child. What is the harm? Your young life is impressed very profoundly by the whole panoply of national life, the pageantry of its institutions, the beauty of its countryside, its literature and its music; and the total effect of all this on you is that you incline to adopt outlooks and attitudes which are typical of your society and your social group. This may not be the way of learning about society which a methodological purist would prefer, but it is the way we encounter life. This is the actual stuff of our experience. Whether or not we start off with a *tabula rasa*, by the time we come to the stage of development when we can examine our beliefs critically, there has been a good deal of scribbling on its surface, some of it almost ineradicable, and much of the scribbling has not been done by us. So, by the time we can examine beliefs to see if they are worthy of acceptance, we already possess many of them and they form a part of our way of looking at things'.

This is to be granted as true, though it doesn't show us a way out of the difficulty. This procedure seems harmless enough when it is spoken of in terms of national heritage, although extremely harmful beliefs have been transmitted by this method, such as the belief that neighbouring States were populated by inferior beings who were our natural enemies. Perhaps this is the place where we should try to clarify our conception of the relationship between belief and authority.

* * *

AUTHORITY AND BELIEF

What do we mean when we say that we believe something? How does believing differ from knowing? St Thomas Aquinas said that when we believe we assent to what is thought (*Credere est cum assensu cogitare*). But we should not assume that he meant voluntary assent, for belief and assent (as this word is usually understood) are quite different. In the oppressive periods of ecclesiasticism it was frequently regarded as a sufficient test of orthodoxy if a man assented to the dogmas of the Church. Belief is a more private matter and is not to be compassed by an act of will. No one can be blamed for believing that the moon is made of green cheese. We 'arrive at' beliefs, or we 'come to believe' or 'prefer to believe' or 'choose to believe', if our ordinary language about belief is to be credited. But in point of fact we ought probably to regard the last two expressions as inexact. They are common expressions, and they imply that belief is voluntary, but surely they are some kind of hyperbole for, 'I find myself believing X, and I am not anxious to endure the pain which I would suffer if I tried to undermine my belief'. If I say, 'I am going to believe in Father Christmas from now on', or 'I am determined to believe in Father Christmas', I am simply expressing unbelief. If there is still any doubt in our minds about this, we might consider what is implied by the expression, 'I wish I could believe', or by 'I wish I didn't believe'. These are both meaningful and common and they assume that our beliefs are not (or not always) voluntary.

If belief is essentially an involuntary attitude, we should expect that a man would not be blamed for his beliefs. If a man believes

LEGITIMACY AND LIMITATIONS

in the inferiority of other nations, we may think it is not a good belief to hold, and we may try to change his belief, but ought we to say that he is wicked to believe it? If belief is involuntary we can hardly condemn him. Neither, of course, can we praise a man for his excellent beliefs.

How do we come to believe the things we do believe? Apparently in a variety of ways, some of which we may know about, while others are unconscious. If I interview an importunate woman who tells me the story of her need, it may not be easy to identify all the factors which determine whether I believe or disbelieve her story, or whether I am left in a state of suspension. (We call this suspension 'indecision', but if the contention about the involuntariness of belief is accepted, I do not decide to believe. When I say, 'I am going to believe you', I may mean that I find myself believing or, more probably, I simply mean that I am going to act as though I believed you.) The nature of the woman's story itself will affect me, but so may her appearance, especially her manner, her voice and her expression—together with my own state of receptiveness or credulity. If I have just been disappointed in my efforts to rehabilitate another applicant for help in whose story I believed, I will probably start with a predisposition to unbelief. In other words, we can have reasons for believing, but the attitude of belief is itself involuntary; and although we discover this attitude in ourselves, it is not certain, or even likely, that we shall be able to discover all the reasons for it.

In what sense, then, can I be said to believe on authority? This cannot mean that I have assented to or accepted a belief because I have been told that I ought to, because we have seen that assent, in this sense, is voluntary, and is an outward profession rather than an attitude. Nor can it mean that I have come to believe because of evidence, for although the very existence of the authority is evidence of a kind, the method of authority and the method of appeal to evidence are quite different; though as we have seen, we may confuse them by using the word 'authority' for what is evidential. But can the expression 'I believe on authority' mean 'I have accepted this authority and so I have tacitly agreed to accept whatever it enjoins'? But this is not belief, it is assent. If I submit to the authority of a Church, confessing my own inability to think out or to select a coherent system of religious ideas for myself, I will not necessarily find myself believing all that it teaches. But the more wholehearted my submission, the more I will be inclined to believe what it tells me to believe. In the end I may come to believe all that it propounds. On the other hand, I may not need to submit in this way if I have been brought up from childhood in an atmosphere of respect for an authority. However this position is reached, we have to recognize that it is a common one. I find myself believing that an authority, whether a defining authority or an authority which claims to tell me what is true and what is untrue, is an infallible source of truth. In that case I shall find myself believing that whatever the authority claims to be true is, in fact, true. But the only guarantee of a truth which is so communicated to me, apart from rational probability, of which we are taking no account, is the well-foundedness of my own original attitude of belief in the authority. The procedure is circular.

So far we have considered belief only in relation to authority. What is to be said about the belief which we form, or which is formed in us, after we have consulted evidence? Does this differ from the belief which we have about authority or the beliefs which are inculcated by authority? It is difficult to see that the belief itself, as an attitude of mind, can be of two or more kinds. We are capable of entertaining rational and irrational beliefs, but the difference between them appears to lie in the mode of their generation. These differently based beliefs differ also in their relationship to truth. A rational belief is more likely to be true if the evidence on which it is based is reliable, and less likely if the evidence is unreliable. In theory, at least, such a rationally based belief is one which can change in content whenever new evidence is presented and assessed. Our irrational beliefs, however, do not yield so easily to contrary evidence. They are less tentative—though there is almost always an element of tentativeness when we use the word 'believe' instead of 'know'. 'I believe' expresses a personal attitude, whereas 'I know', if the words are used with similar emphasis, implies immediacy and certainty in relation to what is known. The tentativeness of belief on evidence is more evident, one would think, than is the case in irrational belief. In other words, a strongly held irrational belief can give us a feeling that is very close to certainty, whereas a strongly held belief founded on evidence retains the feeling of tentativeness to a somewhat greater extent.

As an illustration of this, we have questioned Christians who professed to believe in the literal inerrancy of scripture and have found that the claim of belief is associated with powerful emotions which lend to the believer a feeling akin to certainty—a feeling which they would call 'conviction'. One distinguished Free Church orator whose belief was of this order reported to us that if he dared to question a single word of scripture the whole edifice of his belief would fall down. It was either unexamined all, or nothing. On the other hand, a pathologist, who as a result of a series of experiments in which a specific organism in a mixed culture is killed, comes to believe that he has found a successful anti-bacterial substance deleterious to the organism in question, will not find his belief in ruins if subsequent tests show that the substance does not always destroy the bacterium, or does not do so in isolation. He is not further back in the progress of discovery because he misread earlier evidence and entertained a partly erroneous belief. He is further forward.

It is difficult to be sure, of course, that there are no irrational elements in a supposedly rational belief. If the scientist in question has been publicly acclaimed for his discovery he may have a little more difficulty in perceiving the significance of contrary evidence when it is presented to him.

To return to the question which provoked this discussion; we had considered whether the authority in religion might be regarded as an authority for the will rather than for the intellect and for truth. We saw that this would identify religious authority much more closely with what we thought to be the primary type of authority. But such an authority might be used to influence belief—as it is (consciously or unconsciously) in the inculcation of the beliefs we have about our nation and race. What could be said about the propriety of such a use of authority in religion?

It may be argued that since we have assumed that belief is not voluntary, or largely involuntary, an authority for the will would be largely irrelevant to belief. Hardly so, for although we often have the hardihood to claim that no one else can make up our mind for us, our attitudes seem to be arrived at, quite commonly, by a process of adoption—though perhaps not conscious adoption. Believing may not be an act of will for me, but it is precisely the power of a true authority that it can exercise suasion, and that it is able to secure my compliance. It is able to do that, not by causing me to will this or that, but by impressing or perhaps anaesthetizing my will. When the schoolmaster says 'Sit down!' do I have to will to sit down? One would think not. At the very least, my will is much assisted by the habit of obedience. And if he should say, 'Bulgarians, believe me, are deeply religious and rarely take a bath', do I need any act of will to believe this? Rather would I require an effort of will to submit the matter to scrutiny and keep reasonable doubt alive.

This is surely how we come to believe on authority, once we have either made an initial submission or have grown into the tradition of acceptance. Believing is an attitude of the whole person, and while it may be generated by the evidence of the senses, or by reflection upon evidence, and intensified or diminished by relevant feelings, there would seem to be an implicit inner decision involved in which the will is concerned, though we may not be aware of it. Between 'I do not believe' and 'I do now believe' lies a process of which a probable part is the generally uncontrolled implication of the will—not consciously controlled, that is, by ourselves. But what *we* do not control in belief may well be controlled for us by the imperative of authority.

The fact seems to have emerged that although we have rejected the idea of an infallible authority for truth in religion we must reckon with an authority which not only defines acceptable belief and regulates conduct—we have acknowledged its right in these matters—but also inculcates beliefs upon the sole condition that we place ourselves, or find ourselves, within the orbit of its influence. This is the mechanism by which Plato thought the citizens of the Republic could be induced to believe in the fantastic myth which graded the members of society according to their supposed metallic content. When Socrates has outlined the myth, a story so patently ridiculous that Plato makes him embarrassed in the telling of it, he concludes, 'That is the story. Do you think there is any way of making them believe it?' 'Not in the first generation,' says Glaucon, 'but you may succeed with the second and later generations.'[2]

This state of affairs is neither a good thing nor a bad thing but the unavoidable result of our suggestibility. It is, however, a good reason for scrutinizing the beliefs which we find ourselves holding. If I find myself believing that the Bulgarians are religious and

---

[2] *Republic*, 414-5 (Lee's translation, Penguin Books).

unwashed, I must not shirk the labour of discovering whether there is a justification for my belief; nor can the justification lie in the schoolmaster's statement about the habits of Bulgarians. We have seen that there is no virtue in believing, but there is a difference of value in beliefs, and they are to be valued, not by their orthodoxy, nor by their grandeur, but by their approximation to the truth so far as we are able to discover it.

* * *

AUTHORITY AND FAITH

Since we were led, by the notion of an authority for the will, to consider the relationship of belief and authority, there are some other aspects of the relationship between authority and religious experience which should be considered. How, for instance, is authority in religion related to faith? First, let us see if we can decide what is meant by faith. In the context of the Christian religion faith and belief are partly coincident and partly distinct. It is unfortunate that whilst the noun πίστις is used for 'faith' in the New Testament, the cognate verb is used for both 'to have faith' and 'to believe'. It is perhaps as a consequence of this confusion that there has sometimes been argument at cross purposes about the nature and import of faith. St James declares that there is no virtue in πιστεύειν. The demons also believe the facts concerning God (James 2[19]). But when πιστεύειν is followed by the prepositions εἰς or ἐν, its meaning is changed to signify an attitude of personal trust of a much more voluntary character than belief. Roughly speaking πιστεύειν in relation to facts is 'to believe' but in relation to persons it is 'to trust' or 'to have faith in' them. Certainly this is the difference in meaning which later usage has sanctioned, so that when we speak of belief we speak of an attitude largely involuntary and therefore not to be praised or blamed (as James points out), but when we speak of faith we indicate a partly or even largely voluntary attitude (if these terms are not incompatible with each other) of active entrustment. So it is that in Christian theology the absence of faith tends, rightly or wrongly, to be viewed with disapprobation. In the less careful expositions of some types of Protestantism faith is even presented as a kind of laudable performance which secures the favour of God, whilst in more careful theologies it is thought of as a gift from God. (Cf. Ephesians 2⁸: 'For it is by grace that you are saved, through trusting (διὰ πίστεως) him; it is not your doing. It is God's gift, not a reward for work done' (*New English Bible*).

In the light of this let us consider again our actual use of the word 'faith' and its difference in meaning from 'belief'. We suggested that in faith we do not simply discover an attitude in ourselves (although we may discover the kind of belief which makes faith easier) but we adopt an attitude, and it is an attitude of active, personal reliance. So far as this is an attitude toward God it is recognized, theologically, to be quite distinct. Whatever crucial importance is attached to faith in God is not attached to faith in the authorities which from time to time purport to represent God. We may speak of faith in the Bible or the Church but if we do so the content of the word is weakened, and it is more nearly belief. Traditionally, faith is offered to God not to the Church or the Bible. It may be that the concept of faith and the concept of authority do not go well together. The authority of Church and Bible may be propaedeutic, but if they claim certainty for their deliverances they are not leading us to faith but confronting us with certain knowledge. And whilst certain knowledge of God would not eliminate the possibility of faith as trust, it would mean that all the element of belief must be emptied from it. Without the element of uncertainty, of risk, of self-committal, the traditional notion of faith would be unrecognizable. But if authorities which make such claims cannot afford knowledge which is certain, how can they be infallible? The answer seems to be that if we put our trust in the authority, which 'knows' certainly that its dogmas are true, and we believe what we are told to believe, we shall be believing what is certainly true. But surely this is only another way for the authority to underwrite our faith, and then instead of leaning perilously across the abyss of the Christian mysteries we find ourselves on the solid roadway of an irrefrangible bridge. But does this not imply that if we have faith in God in the first place we do not need an authority which guarantees the content of faith? Or does it mean that if we put our trust in such an authority, and accept its guarantees, we misconceive what it is to have faith in God? We are like travellers who go to be carried over the river by the fabulous Christopher, but who first take the precaution of learning to swim.

Our account of this, however, is unsatisfactory in at least two respects. First, it is not to be assumed that the only way in which we can speak of faith as 'the gift of God' is to regard it as a state of mind mysteriously produced within us by God. Second, we shall be flying in the face of the facts if we deny that faith in God is evoked and supported by Church and Bible.

Let us consider these statements in reverse order. In what way can faith be said to be evoked or supported by authority and yet not (for this was our former objection) guaranteed? Can we not regard the Bible and the Church as evidential authority—the only kind of authority which we could see to be relevant to the task of discovering what is true? In that case, we encounter in the deliverances of Bible and Church a revelation which may be of God (not one which must be of God) and also an invitation to faith in God transmitted by those who have not only an investigable claim to mediate the invitation of God, but who themselves speak from a long tradition which enables them to know, with a wider empirical reference, what are the consequences of a life of faith. For the Church to possess such an authority is not to possess infallibility, but it is not a negligible thing to be the bearer of a living tradition. We would be inclined to regard this as the most profound sense in which the Church can be said to possess authority. Furthermore, if the Bible is regarded as the source book to which the living tradition must always be referred, and the only explicit witness for the cardinal events of the Gospel and for the acts and words of Christ, it will be honoured much more than it ever would be by the superstitious regard of those who have insisted that it is an infallible literary oracle.

On this view we have in Bible and Church the data of faith and an account of its nature as a living attitude and experience. Once we have seen the possibility of this kind of authority, it is easier to see in what sense faith could be reasonably thought of as a gift of God, without an undue attenuation of our share in it. The authority of the Church and the Bible lies in their value as sources for fact and experience, and their exercise of that authority is not (or should not be) imperatival, and certainly not imperatival in relation to truth. The authority is proclamatory. Their claim, moreover, is that the proclamation is originally from God and therefore our response to it, the response of faith, is a response to God's action. Without this primary self-revealing activity of God, the response of faith would be impossible and, in this sense at least, faith can be spoken of as a gift of God.

*   *   *

AUTHORITY AND DECISION

If faith has a more voluntary character than belief, the third word we shall mention in this trilogy of individual religious experience, 'decision', is presumably more clearly voluntary than faith. It stands for the extreme assertion of the autonomy of the self in religion. In the last resort every question is settled for us, every action determined for us, or so we may care to think, by our decision. This, say existentialists like Jaspers, is the distinctiveness of our selfhood. The 'authentic self' as distinct from the merely empirical self, is characterized by this power to make decisions. Whatever else we are not, we are the decision makers. We can set out to undermine any authority by reminding it that the decision which constitutes it or recognizes it is ours. Its deliverances of truth, so far as we are concerned, possess no authentification which is valid without the decision by which we come to regard it and accept it as authority.

All of which seems to make very little difference to the extreme forms of authority in religion. 'Your only decision', they seem to say, 'is to stop deciding for yourself. Make your submission. That decision we will allow you. That does not constitute us as authority, it merely recognizes that a *de facto* authority already exists. After that, we will make the essential decisions for you, so far as truth is concerned, and we will tell you not only how to behave, but what to believe.' This method does not rule out intelligence, but it limits the problems which confront it. It does not preclude moral effort, but it saves the time and energy we might otherwise waste in trying to decide which course we ought to adopt. Decision does involve effort, and it seems to be rather a painful and costly activity which we are glad to escape when escape is honourably possible. Doesn't the method of authority in religion relieve us from most of the painful hours of indecision that are the usual prelude to our major decisions in other fields—if not from all of them?

In these two paragraphs there are a number of assertions which we must examine a little more carefully. First of all, how true is it that I have this decision-making character? We are all convinced that we make some decisions but dare we ask, without raising the whole question of the freedom of the will, whether there are not other factors in decision besides my will? In each decision I am confronted by the matter upon which I must decide—I have a choice to make. Next, in most cases, I must exercise judgement, however rudimentary, and then I must make up my mind. But is my final act of choice unaffected by everything except my judgement? For that matter is my judgement unaffected by anything except the matters submitted to judgement?

We have come to know ourselves well enough to discard any over-optimistic estimates of our freedom. But if 'indeterminism' is to be ruled out, it follows that all my judgements and my consequent decisions must be affected by factors which are extraneous to the matter under consideration and possibly irrelevant, or at least not known to be relevant. This is a situation in which we have now learnt to make decisions with great cheerfulness. We take what safeguards we can against the possibility that unconscious factors are prompting a wrong decision (they may be prompting a right one, of course) and make the best of our unideal mechanisms. But if we are not aware of all the factors which help to constitute the totality of our experience at the moment of decision, can the decision really be called ours? Or is it a decision at all? What do we conclude about the behaviour of the hypnotic subject who is told that after he awakes, upon a given sign, he will remove a flower-pot from the table and put it behind the settee—and who, in doing so, assures us that he has just decided that the sun is shining too brightly on the table? Was the subsequent decision to remove the flowers a real decision or a pseudo-decision? It is difficult to see how the possible degrees of reality could be assessed.

It is clear, however, that some decisions are more likely than others to be influenced in this way. If I am called upon to decide upon a suitable site for an aerodrome, unconscious factors are unlikely to have very serious weight, although they will have some. There are no local gods to propitiate nowadays—or not many. Level ground is needed, not too near mountains, as free as possible from fogs, with good land communications, and so on. But if I am deciding about the religious education of my children, how real is my decision in comparison? It is understandable that it must be to some extent preformed by relevant previous decisions and that I can allow for; but the whole field of my religious opinions, prejudices, superstitions and fears is invoked by the need to make such a decision. Moreover, if I am already attached to a religious system, or even have lived my life within the influence of one, what we found to be true about the power to induce belief will probably be effective in relation to my decisions, which to a large extent must depend on my beliefs. If this is true, it seems likely that a good many religious matters which we assume have been decided by us, have been the result of decisions preformed, more or less, by the systems of authority to which we belong. This we would expect to be true for all decisions made in the context of religious belief, but more significant in effect where we are under the influence of rigid or powerful forms of authority. In many cases the preforming of decision is overt, and there is scarcely any decision to be made—unless, perhaps, it is the confirmatory decision to obey authority in a new situation. An example which comes to mind is the case of a member of the sect called Jehovah's Witnesses who may be advised that his child needs a blood transfusion. A member of that organization may not have such a transfusion or permit it to his children for fear of committing a 'sin', the sin of 'mixing blood'. For every decision like this which is obviously taken out of people's hands by authority, there must be many others where few of us are conscious, or fully conscious, of the influence of authority.

So much for the influence of authority upon decision. It is not the only extraneous influence, of course. Presumably we can best guard against the possibility of irrational decisions by making our relationship with authority as clear to ourselves as possible. At least we shall then know the approximate extent of our attachment and some of the reasons for it, and the probable bearing of authority upon our individual decisions will be more evident.

If we must be under authority it is as well to realize, so far as possible, the extent of our compliance and the rationale of the authority system to which we belong. A Roman Catholic need not accept with closed eyes the directions of his church which discourage mixed marriages. It is his duty to discover why mixed marriages are frowned upon, and to relate this to the whole system of belief which authority commends to him. It may be true, as we have suggested, that no man can make a completely uninfluenced decision, but no man may abrogate his selfhood and his moral responsibility by surrendering his power to decide. At least he must share in the decisions which are proper to him, and the plea that he has not shared in them, but only complied with authority, cannot diminish his responsibility for the consequences.

Another problem stems from one of the statements about authority and decision which prefaced this discussion. It concerns the part played in the constitution of authority by our decision to submit to a particular authority. To what extent are we then the authority for the authority, or to what extent are we confronted by a *de facto* authority? Let us suppose that I decide that the doctrines of the Orthodox Church are those with which I can agree, and thereafter join that church. In doing so I accept and bind myself to her credal statements. If I am now challenged as to the truth of these statements, can I plead that they are true because they are delivered by authority, when the authority would not have existed for me unless I had chosen it? There is a misconception here which arises from the confusion between authority for truth and authority for the will. This has already been discussed at some length. It should be enough to remember that the truth relationship is not imperatival—I cannot submit to an authority 'for truth' and then have truth constituted for me or guaranteed for me by the authority. There could be no word of command so that what was not known to be true previously is, after the imperative has been spoken, to be regarded as indubitably true. This kind of activity is proper to an authority for the will, and it is to regulate conduct, not somehow to expostulate truth. As far as truth is concerned, what I receive in the way of direction from authority must depend upon the wisdom of my choice. From authority as a system of discipline I will receive directions about such things as marriage or blood transfusion. But presumably I will investigate the range of disciplinary regulations before I put myself in the position where I am expected to comply; though if new regulations are framed and accepted by the authority I will be bound by them, unless I can withdraw from the system altogether. But if new statements about what is true are made by the authority, I shall have no reason for believing that they are true simply because my chosen authority has pronounced them to be so. It seems to be the case, then, that when I decide upon an 'authority for truth', I decide what I am going to accept as true—and what I hope to believe. Unless I then leave it to the chosen authority to justify its pronouncements as true (which is not the method of authority), the basis of its authority for truth, as far as I am concerned, cannot be anything which does not depend on the reasons I had for my decision to accept its authority. It would be nonsense for me to say: 'The doctrine of justification by faith is true because it is implied in the Epistle to the Romans, and I do not accept the authority of the Bible.' It is only true for me, on the ground of authority, if I accept such an authority, and then only true in the sense that it is the deliverance of an authority whose pronouncements I regard as true. This circularity in the appeal to the declaratory authority of scripture is well-known, and so is the equally circular device to evade it, which claims that scripture is self-authenticating.

Is there no sense, then, in which we can form a legitimate conception of an authority which is *de facto*, and which does not wait upon our decision? Those who approach the Christian Faith find themselves faced, to some extent, by a living authority in the experience of other Christians and in the communicated impact of the historical events which Christians regard as decisive for faith. There is an authority of a kind here, which might be distinguishable from the authority which regulates societies or which transmits neutral communications in the manner of scholarly authority.

A difficulty about authority so conceived is that it is subtle rather than simple, and Christians have felt the need for an authority which is as plain to descry as it is unambiguous in its dealings with us. We can feel some sympathy for the non-intellectual worshipper who is pushed away from his authorities by reasoning which is impressive, but which he cannot easily follow. In the event he is being treated just as arbitrarily as he would be by the 'truth-telling' of infallible authority. There is an undoubted need for some sort of epexegetic authority in religion. Something a little more pointed and pre-digested is needed than is provided in science by what is called scientific authority. There are, one hopes, no ignorant scientists, but there are many ignorant Christians.

* * *

SUMMARY AND CONCLUSIONS

Despite the dangers which attend generalization, it would seem desirable that some broad statements should be made about the historical narrative of the first three chapters. The narrative of the fourth chapter, concerned as it was with philosophers was traced forward in its theological connexions, but the earlier part of the history should perhaps be seen more clearly in relationship with what follows.

The first part of the history illustrates, so we believe, the most important single fact about religious authority as it is and not as we think it ought to be. The notion of sovereignty in Christianity, of power to rule the minds of others, we would derive not so much from the sovereignty of Christ or the concept of the Kingdom of God, but from the authority forms of human sovereignty. It is for theology to say whether there is a scheme of authority in the New Testament which would explain why later Christians felt that they had a right not only to proclaim their message, but to command, to rule, to punish, in the name of the message. If Jesus really said, as Matthew and Luke report, 'You know that in the world, rulers lord it over their subjects, and their great men make them feel the weight of authority; but it shall not be so with you. Among you whoever wants to be great must be your servant' (Matthew 20^{25f}, *New English Bible*), He would seem to have repudiated in advance any possible claim of temporal power which His disciples may decide to advance either on the basis of their spiritual influence or their relationship with Him. As things turned out, however, the spiritual authority of the Church, while it claimed to be like that of the Apostles, found its expression, in the long run, in terms of human sovereignty, both in the monarchical internal authority of the Church, and the external temporal authority to which the Church successfully aspired. When the grand imperatival authority of the Church was secured in temporal matters, it became easier than ever to assume that truth was also something to be delivered and accepted on authority.

The Greeks had once broken through this awkward alliance between temporal power and so-called 'truth-telling' authority, and had established the claim of free investigation to be the primary means of discovering what is true. But the Greeks also had their difficulties about the problem of authority. We saw that Plato toyed with the idea of some kind of ideal history which should be directive, and should be employed to reinforce a system of authority. The Christian Church claimed to have the custody of such a history, which it did not have to invent, but to inherit and transmit. It was in a position to dress the philosopher-king in a mitre and, before long, to put a sword in his hand. We have seen that Plato appeared to be embarrassed by this contrivance of authority. Both Plato and Aristotle saw that authority was an imperfect device, but they pointed out that it could be used to shape men and societies. The Christian Church, at its official level, took the hint. Afterwards, as we saw, the power factor in the authority of the Church grew in the centuries of conflict when it seemed inconceivable that right could ever manage without might.

It is not difficult to see how easily such a transformation of authority can take place in a religious society. What Reger called 'charismatic' authority, the authority which rests on the giftedness or prowess of the individual (or, according a more specifically Christian connotation of the charisma, on the presence of the gifts of God in him), one would take to be the 'natural' authority in religion. That is to say, this type of authority would be proper to the inspired prophet or to a personality of deep saintliness, just as the authority of command is proper to the gifted warrior. Authority conferred by the charisma does, however, raise problems. It is not transferable; at least, not by a transaction of authority. The kind of charismatic authority which was wielded by Jesus has been wielded by many men since His time, and by some before Him, but its presence in any particular individual is not predictable. One cannot consecrate a bishop and guarantee that this authority will be his in practice—though it will be his in theory. Moreover it seems to be true that as the Church developed it became normal for men of special bent or character to apply themselves to the form of service which suited them best. Thus, the brighter spirits and their followers divided into groups of ability and interest. Some men found satisfaction in a life of scholarship, others in a life of worship and contemplation, others like St Francis, in practical saintliness, while others drifted, or marched, into the tasks of administration. Ideally, of course, the Church is administered by saints, and the charisma is the prime source of their authority. It is a gift of God which ensures the proper discharge of their office. In point of fact, however, the administrators have not possessed such gifts, and it has been found expedient to guarantee the effectiveness of authority by substituting an authority based on the model of monarchy. This can be transferred to legally-appointed successors with less uncertainty than the charisma, which did not observe the precedences of clerical succession. It might bloom in an obscure Irish monk and completely bypass half a dozen popes. The problem still remains. The blessings of Heaven do not always fall where the hand of man appoints, yet some sort of continuity must be secured for the authority of the Church. It might be thought that it would be possible to choose for the responsibility of office those in whom such gifts have been manifested. This has been done. It was done in the case of Augustine, in that of Gregory and Anselm, and there have been men like William Temple in our own time whose gifts have marked them out for high office in the Church. The strange thing is that prophetic or saintly gifts may not in themselves commend a man for office. Practical abilities, the power of organization, and sagacity in council, are also important and may in some circumstances be thought to be of prime importance.

Perhaps it may be concluded that the less exciting gifts of administration are not any less the gifts of God and are therefore a proper basis for choice. But the possessors of the charisma are not chosen so much as recognized. And while the clever administrators may possess gifts of administration, their authority does not lie in their gifts, but in the power and rule which has been entrusted to them.

In any case, we should be deluding ourselves if we were to assume that the succession of authority in the Church was determined by either charismatic qualities or competence to rule, or both. Simony, royal favour, and the consideration due to members of one's own family, are only some of the dismal instruments which have been used in the transfer of ecclesiastical rule.

It may be significant for a juster evaluation of the authority of the Church that it preserved in its spiritual and intellectual life, through men like John the Scot, Roger Bacon, and many less distinguished members of the rank and file (and not a few princes of the Church too) the seeds of a recovery of spiritual freedom. This was partly a heritage from the Greeks, but partly it was something held in common with the Greeks. The self-renewal of the Church after the Dark Ages came only partly from without. From this time onward the Church bore within itself the developing impetus of critical thought and submitted to a certain amount of critical self-examination. The system of authority as it had been developed, however, could not settle down comfortably side by side with the speculative and critical activity with which it had perforce to coexist for a time. After some period of strain, the break came at the Reformation. This was not a simple conflict of doctrine with doctrine, or of philosophy with religion, but the expression of a deep hunger for new ways of living, for new relationships, and for freedom to explore the new knowledge which was already half disclosed to the eyes of Western Christendom.

The rest of our story concerned the use to which speculative freedom was put once it was secured. The restraint of authority was partly removed, and from some men it was removed altogether, but we saw that the efforts men made to manage without authority in religion were not too successful. Technical and practical difficulties arose which cast doubt on the ability of reason to do all that was asked of it, and for some Christians, this was the signal to look again for the apparent stability and non-rational direction afforded by a system of authority.

The history we have recalled holds all the ingredients of the modern situation so far as authority in religion is concerned. It displays the effect of reliance upon Book, Church or prophetic charisma, and it holds its own warning about the consequences of failing to find a working solution. Ecclesiastical authority as peremptory, sovereign, and necessary by definition, has shown a few of its paces and one would think that Western civilization is not likely to encourage a repeat performance. Against such excessive authority, individualism was the extremity of protest, while as an anchorage for those who found stability impossible without authority, the Bible was the obvious choice as a stabilizer. But biblicism is a tyranny of the mind no less than ecclesiasticism, and if our only other refuge in religion is to trust in the 'authority' of each man's private revelation, or imaginings, or convictions, our case will be unenviable. We have considered some of the attempts which have been made to present religious authority in forms which would preserve the intellectual negotiability of theological postulation, so that the problems of religion can be discussed intelligently in the presence of other disciplines.

We found a suggestive value in Martineau's idea of a moral authority in Christianity, speaking rather to the will than to the intellect. The same suggestion was noticed in Forsyth, together with a quite remarkable prefiguring of the neo-orthodoxy of the present time which has revalued the Bible and contrives to regard it as the Word of God without regarding it as the words of God. Oman regarded personal vision, in the corroborating society of other Christians, as the apex of authority; but this is hardly satisfactory unless we decide that we will have to manage without authority. The method of personal vision, or subjective experience, or corporate vision, is defensible, but it is to be regarded as a substitute for authority rather than a provision of an alternative authority. When we speak of the authority of the prophet we do not refer to his own certainty or the subjective reason for his certainty, but to his power to sway others to the adoption of his view-point.

For the most part, the modified forms of religious authority at which we looked were concerned with a new attitude to the Bible and its background, and with new ways of regarding and co-ordinating individual experience. In the case of Barth, though his theology is dominated by 'the Word of God', a place has also been found for a greatly enhanced view of the authority of the Church and of dogma. Otherwise, we have not considered suggestions for a new ecclesiastical authority. The original problem was to limit the authority of the Church, to avoid narrow and superstitious views of the Bible, and still to emerge with a workable authority which would deliver Christians from over-enthusiastic individualism and afford them intellectual freedom without depriving their faith of a reasonable foundation.

Much of the ensuing discussion has been necessarily critical. It has seemed to many people that the old authorities in religion were unsatisfactory, but to mend them, or to substitute better ones, has proved almost insuperably difficult. The difficulty continues, but our study seems to have disclosed some hope that the problem is not insoluble, especially if we are prepared to look carefully at the meanings we attach to the word 'authority' when we use it in a religious context, and if we are prepared to make some attempt to modify its meaning by a more scrupulous usage.

We have suggested that the word 'authority' is better regarded as metaphorical whenever its fundamental imperatival connotation is inappropriate, and we have argued that it is inappropriate when we are speaking of the transmission of truth, though still appropriate for the ordering of a society and for the regulation of conduct with an agreed framework of social convention. (This imperatival usage may be legitimately wider in general society, but a Church can only tell its people what they *must* do as Christians, and when it speaks to the world it can only indicate what others ought to do, which is to give guidance rather than to exercise authority.)

The concession of regulative authority cannot stand alone, however, as a satisfactory solution, because the primary need has been to discover something which may, with propriety, be regarded as a suitable mode of authority for the truths which Christianity proclaims. We have argued that such an authority cannot be a guarantee of truth, but we have also seen that the need of the individual for a basis for his belief, faith, and decision, is not the need for a guarantee. His need is rather for an authority which is annunciatory and evocative, one which must be heard rather than one which cannot be disbelieved. This authority already exists in the distinctive Christian message of the Bible and in the corporate experience and witness of the Church. To distinguish what is essential in this authority from what is incidental, or even erroneous, is a task for scholarship and piety rather than for an infallible referee—even then finality may not be attained. But does this matter so long as the task of this authority would be to evoke faith rather than to convey infallible information?

It may be objected that even if we cannot recognize in authority that which tells us what we must believe, it is not sufficient for the purposes of the Christian Faith that all we can discover is an authority which we may believe. That would go no farther than the intellectual authority provided for scientists by scientists. There is a 'must' in scientific authority, but it is only that we must take account of what is delivered to us as scientists by scientists. So much is easily conceded to the authority which we have suggested would be better called the 'testimony' of the Bible and the Church. Is this concept of authority enough for the needs of theology? This, in fact, is probably a question which need not concern the present inquiry. It is a question for theology. We have tried to limit ourselves to a survey of some of the factors which would enable us to understand the authority relationship, and to a discussion which was largely concerned to find out in what sense it is reasonable to think of an authority in religion.

LEGITIMACY AND LIMITATIONS 153

There is one more suggestion which may or may not prove fruitful to theology. Every study of this kind is aided or hampered by the initial conceptions of the writer. He begins, perhaps not always with conclusions to which his argument will move, but with an individual way of looking at his subject. We approached this discussion with the unexamined conviction that the thing which had to be considered, examined and analysed was authority, as an objective fact. Later, this attitude was modified as it became apparent that what we were dealing with was not authority as an isolable entity, but a relationship which we came to know as the authority relationship, a relationship which we could know about from our involvement in it. It became evident, as we discussed the relationship of the individual to authority in religious experience, that it might be possible to regard and classify authority in terms of the reaction or effect which it produces. This might provide a useful point of vantage from which to survey authority. If this view were adopted, it would be possible to recognize what we took to be the original and peremptory sort of authority, because it would provoke the response of obedience or compliance. If the tribal leader says, 'Kneel down!' or, 'Fight my enemies!' we obey, or take the consequences. So, in a sense, we know what kind of authority has addressed us by the response which it seeks to elicit.

The authority to which the scholar or scientist refers does not demand obedience or compliance, but only scrutiny; only that it should be taken account of or consulted. Again, we can recognize this type of authority by the type of response it invites. Let us consider, then, what response appears to be invited by religious authority. To some extent the response is one of obedience, but we felt this to be justifiable only as a response to a disciplinary authority, whether of Church or community. The response is also to scrutinize, to consult, as in the case of scientific authority, for many matters are reported by the informatory tradition which exists in a Church, and their value is manifestly uneven. If the Bible is to be regarded as having authority it must, to some extent, be authority of this kind. For example, a document offered to us by Christian piety is found to advise that jealous husbands who suspect their wives of infidelity, on grounds however slender, should submit their wives to trial by ordeal. If poison, administered by a priest, does not kill them, they may be regarded as innocent. One would hope that it is fairly evident that we are not expected to respond obediently to primitive custom of this order. The most we can do is to take note of the fact that such a custom is reported (in Numbers 5^{14ff}) and to add it to the material we have for a history of the way in which religious and moral ideas have developed.

The two types of response mentioned so far are clearly present in religion, but they do not, taken together, suffice to indicate the totality of the response which religious authority elicits. The chief area of response is probably indicated by words like those which we have already considered in relation to authority: belief, faith and decision. Of these, perhaps the third could be omitted when we are considering what is the distinctive response to religious authority. We decided previously that if our decision is 'on authority' it is not really decision at all, and in considering authority from the viewpoint of response this kind of 'decision' would come under the heading of obedience. Moreover, in so far as decision is not on authority, but arises from our own deliberation, it can only be called a response to authority in a secondary sense. If I have come to a decision about a statement offered to me by the Bible or the Church, then my decision concerns authority, but it is not on authority. At the most, religious decision is a secondary response arising from faith or belief or conviction, the preconditions of which may have been aroused in me by authority.

It would seem, then, that we have still to account for an authority which would be able to elicit the response of belief or faith, and that there is a likelihood that such an authority exists in religion, apart from the authority which demands obedience and that which simply imparts information. Our examination of the meaning of belief led us to think that an authority for belief must be persuasive; that it must be, to some extent, what Forsyth and Martineau called an authority for the will. Yet it would have to be an authority which inclined without coercing, for belief must still represent our own judgement if it is to be of value for us—we would not be able to value irrational belief if we judged it to be irrational and unlikely to be true. Our faith, moreover, must include a voluntary content if it is to be credited to us, even in part, and not wholly credited to the authority which calls it forth. For though theologians speak of faith, with Paul, as a gift of God, they still seem to regard it as being our faith. To say that it is given to us is surely to say that God acts so as to evoke the response of faith (or of non-faith), so that the initiating action is God's and not ours.

We appear to be looking for an authority which is evocative rather than overtly peremptory or merely expository. In the terms in which we expressed this before, something to fill the gap which otherwise exists between the authority which we must obey and the authority which we may believe. This, if we could identify it, would be the *de facto* authority which does not entirely wait upon our decision concerning the merits of authority but which meets us as an external reality which, while it may not be decisive for our belief or faith, is effectively evocative.

Let it be noted, again, that the existence of an authority of this type has been suggested to us by the facts of belief and faith—not any belief and faith, but the long and obstinate and mostly fruitful history of Christian response as belief and faith. Then let us recall our conclusion about the legitimate concepts of an authority for religion which remain to us when borrowed and inappropriate notions of authority have been rejected. We suggested that in addition to disciplinary and expository or informatory authority, there might be a third type of authority which meets us in the life of the Church, both present and past, and in the impact of the dogmatically basic events of Christian history. These come to us as a presentation, so far as truth is concerned, and only as an imperative, or a directive, so far as our conduct is concerned. They meet us as evidence, but evidence which is concentrated and systematized and 'lived in'. It would be understandable if Christians were to feel that such presentations have a greater evocative power than their more random encounters with systems and phenomena which invite attention or assent. They are no longer neutral presentations. It may be true, as we have suggested, that they can carry no guarantee of truth, but that is no loss if what is needed is an evocative basis for religious experience.

BIBLIOGRAPHY

Works referred to in the text, or consulted

Greek Philosophy, Thales to Plato, J. Burnet (Macmillan, 1914).
Ancient Greek Religion, H. J. Rose (Hutchinson).
Plato, *The Republic, The Apology.*
Aristotle, *Politics, Metaphysics.*
Hebrew Religion, Oesterley and Robinson (S.P.C.K., 1930).
The Cambridge Ancient History, Vol. I (Cambridge University Press, 1923).
Greek Thought and the Origin of the Scientific Spirit, Robin (Kegan Paul, Trench, Trubner & Co. Ltd, 1928).
The Philosophy of Greece, A. W. Benn (Grant Richards, 1898).
A Study of History, A. J. Toynbee (Abridgement by Somervell, Vol. II, Oxford, 1957).
The Shorter Cambridge Medieval History, Vols I and II (C.U.P., 1952).
The Cambridge Modern History, Vol. I (C.U.P., 1902).
The Dark Ages, Charles Oman (Rivington, 1919).
History of the Christian Churches, A. R. Whitham (Rivington, 1931).
The Rise and Influence of Rationalism in Europe, W. E. H. Lecky (Longmans, Green & Co., 1910).
The Birth of the Middle Ages, Moss (Oxford, 1935).
History of Medieval Philosophy, Vol. I, Maurice de Wolf, trans. Messenger (Nelson, 1952).
Authority and Reason in the Early Middle Ages, A. J. Macdonald (Oxford, 1933).
Essays in Liberality, A. R. Vidler (S.C.M., 1957)
Spiritual Authority in the Church of England, E. C. Rich (Longmans, 1953).
The Authority of Scripture, J. K. S. Reid (Methuen, 1957).
Fundamentalism and the Church of God, Gabriel Hebert (S.C.M., 1957).
An Existentialist Theology, John Macquarrie (S.C.M., 1955).
New Essays in Philosophical Theology, Flew and Macintyre (S.C.M., 1955).
Mystery and Philosophy, Michael B. Foster (S.C.M., 1957).
An Analysis of Knowing, John Hartland-Swann (Allen and Unwin, 1958).
The Nature of Metaphysical Thinking, D. M. Emmett, (Macmillan, 1945).
Philosophical Analysis, J. O. Urmson (Oxford, 1956).
Bacon, *Philosophical Works,* ed. Robertson (Routledge, 1905).
Descartes, *Discourse of Method, Meditations, Principles* (Blackwood, 1925).

Hobbes, *Leviathan*, Everyman Edition.
Hobbes, Richard Peters (Pelican Books, 1956).
Leibniz, *Discourse and Correspondence with Arnauld* (Open Court, Illinois, 1950).
Leibniz, *Philosophical Writings*, Everyman Edition.
Leibniz, *The Monadology* (Latta, Oxford, 1898).
Metaphysical Beliefs, Alasdair Macintyre (S.C.M., 1957).
Contemporary Philosophy, F. Copleston (Burns and Oates, 1956).
Retreat from Truth, C. R. G. Mure (Blackwell, 1958).
Authority, edited by Carl J. Friedrich (Harvard, 1958).
The Seat of Authority in Religion, J. Martineau (Longmans, Green and Co., 1890).
Vision and Authority, John Oman (Hodder and Stoughton, 2nd edn, 1928).
Authority and Freedom, R. H. Thouless (Hodder and Stoughton, 1954).
Christian Theology and Natural Science, E. L. Mascall (Longmans, 1956).
The Problem of Knowledge, A. J. Ayer(Macmillan, 1956).
Types of Modern Theology, H. R. Mackintosh (Nisbet, 1937).
A History of Freedom of Thought, J. B. Bury (Oxford, 2nd edn, 1952).
Reason and Anti-reason in our Time, Karl Jaspers (S.C.M., 1952).
History of Philosophy from Thales to Compte, G. H. Lewes (Longmans, Green and Co., 1880).
The Philosophy of Kant, selected and translated Watson (Maclehose, Glasgow, 1901).
History of Philosophy, W. Windelband (Macmillan, 1923).
Students History of Philosophy, A. K. Rogers (Macmillan, New York, 3rd edn, 1935).
A Hundred Years of Philosophy, John Passmore (Duckworth, 1957).
Apollinarianism, C. E. Raven (Cambridge, 1923).
History of English Philosophy, W. R. Sorley (Cambridge, 1920).
Reid's Essays on the Intellectual Powers of Man, ed. Woozley (Macmillan, 1941).
The Idea of Revelation in Recent Thought, John Baillie, (Oxford, 1956).
The Travail of Religious Liberty, R. H. Bainton (Lutterworth Press, 1953).
How the Catholic Church is Governed, Heinrich Sharp (Herder-Nelson, 1960).
The Problem of Authority in the Continental Reformers, Rupert Davies (Epworth Press, 1946).
Studies in Religion, Henry Bett (Epworth Press, 1929).
The Letters of John Wesley, Standard Edition (Epworth Press).
The Journal of John Wesley, Standard Edition (Epworth Press).
Ideas of Revelation, H. D. Macdonald (Macmillan, 1959).

BIBLIOGRAPHY

Natural Religion and Christian Theology, C. E. Raven (Cambridge, 1953).
English Thought 1860–1900, The Theological Aspect, L. E. Elliott Binns (Longmans, Green & Co., 1956).
Kant, *Metaphysic of Ethics*, tr. Abbott (Longmans, 10th edn, 1946).
For Faith and Freedom, Leonard Hodgson (Gifford Lectures, Blackwell, Oxford, 1956).
Hume's Dialogues Concerning Natural Religion, ed. Kemp Smith (Nelson, 1947).
The Theory of Economic and Social Organization, Max Weber (William Hodge & Co., tr. by Henderson and Talcott Parsons, 1947).
Dogmatics, Hermann Diem, Oliver and Boyd, 1959.
German Protestantism Since Luther, A. L. Drummond (Epworth Press, 1951).
Church Dogmatics, Karl Barth, English tr., (T. & T. Clarke).

INDEX

Abelard, 30
Absolute, the, 67
Academy, 14
Aether, 101
Alexandrian doctrine, 14
American Constitution, 5
Anaxagoras, 6
Anaximander, 1
Anaximines, 1
Anglicanism, 82
Anselm of Canterbury, 25, 30
Antiochene doctrine, 14
Antiquarianism, 28
Antiqui Doctores, 25
Apostles, 60
Aquinas, 27, 30, 85, 134
Archimedes, 40
Arendt, 92
Arians, 20, 59
Aristotle, 11f, 27, 28, 36, 43, 45, 93, 148
Arminian Magazine, 62
Arnauld, 42
Assumption, dogma of, 106ff
Atomism, 1
Auctoritas, 92f
Authority,
  of the adept, 21
  for belief, 134ff
  and certainty, 112
  charismatic, 99, 112, 148f
  of Christ, 74
  conflicting, 30
  constitutional, 12
  and decision, 142ff, 154
  de facto, 142, 146
  definitions of, 92ff
  ecclesiastical, 17ff, 57ff, 105ff, 148ff
  episcopal, 58
  evocative, 155
  expert, 100ff
  of the facts, 35, 41, 48, 100ff
  and faith, 139ff
  of God, 23f
  of the Good, 11
  institutional, 105f
  internal, 70
  legal-rational, 99
  legitimate, 127ff
  of the ministry, 37
  misplaced, 133
  for morals, 77f
  nature of, 97ff
  papal, 57f
  of the past, 39
  prophetic, 102f
  and reason, 23f, 76, 125f
  scientific, 100f
  of sovereign, 36f
  of scripture, 23f, 26f, 33, 58f, 70f, 109ff, 113f, 122ff
  spiritual, 31f, 76, 103
  and truth, 43, 102ff, 119f, 129, 141
  Vision and, 71ff
  for the will, 76, 118, 129ff, 137f, 153

Babylon, 3
Bacon, Francis, 22, 31ff, 41, 61
Bacon, Roger, 27
Bailey, John, 85, 86
Bainton, 55
Barth, 77, 85, 87, 88, 123ff, 151
Bentham, 78
Belief, 134ff
Berdyaev, 88
Berengar, 26
Berkeley, 32, 48
Bett, Henry, 62
Bible, 79, 82ff, 109ff
Biblical theology, 84ff
Brunner, 77
Bruno, 29, 31
Buber, 88
Bultmann, 88, 89
Burnet, 7

Caesaropapism, 17
Calvin, 60
Cambridge Ancient History, 3
Cambridge Medieval History, 17, 18
Cambridge Platonists, 64
Carolingian Renaissance, 26
Categories of experience, 87
Catholic Church, 78
Certainty, 40, 42, 74, 114f
Chillingworth, 83
Christian Science, 80, 108, 109
Christology, 14
Chrysostom, 17
Clement of Alexandria, 14
Cogito ergo sum, 40
Coleridge, S. T., 67, 124
Compte, 53
Constantine, 17, 22

INDEX

Constantinople, 28
Copplestone, 89, 90

Darius, 2
Davies, R., 58ff
Decision, 142ff
Democritus, 13
Descartes, 35, 38ff, 44, 47, 51, 53f, 88, 91
Drummond, 124f, 129
Doubt, 42, 48

Egoistic basis of society, 36
Empiricism, 24, 41, 47, 52
Enthusiasm, 62, 112
Epicureans, 13
Erigena, 23
Ethics and induction, 32
Eucharistic controversy, 26
Existentialism, 87ff
Existenz, 88

Faith, 59, 106f, 139ff
Fichte, 52f
Forsyth, 74, 85, 118f, 130, 151
Freedom, 5, 9ff, 19, 23ff, 50, 72, 79
Friedrich, 92, 97
Fundamentalism, 8off, 110

Gaiseric, 20
Galileo, 42, 50
Gelasius, 18
Germanic tribes, 20
Good, the, 11
Guarantee, 113ff, 127, 141

Harnack, 71
Hebert, 80
Hedonism, 78
Hegel, 31, 51, 67
Heidegger, 87f
Hincmar, 23
Hobbes, 35ff, 54, 96
Hodgson, L., 84, 90
Hoebel, 94, 97
Huizinga, 29
Humanism, 53
Hume, 47ff, 52, 56, 91f
Hunneric, 20

Idealism, 52f, 66
Ideas, 48f
Impressions, 48f
Inductive method, 32, 35, 54
Infallibility, 72, 106ff
Inner light, 62, 73, 111
Instinct, 95
Intuitionism, 77f
Israel, 3f, 102f

Jaspers, 86, 142

Jesus, religion of, 79, 121
Juvenal, Bertrand de, 93f, 97, 100

Kant, 31, 50ff, 67, 75, 86
Kenosis, 76
Kimbal Young, 95
Knox, 82

Lanfranc, 26
Law, William, 62
Lecky, 16, 18, 20
Leibniz, 39, 43ff, 53, 54, 65
Liberalism, theological, 66f, 70f, 83
Lewes, 24
Locke, 31, 43, 47, 55
Luther, 58ff

Macdonald, A. J., 23, 25, 26
Macdonald, H. D., 63, 65
Macquarrie, 89
Majesterium, 108
Marcel, 88, 89
Martineau, 67f, 77ff, 121f, 150
Mary, the Virgin, 106f
Moderni, 25
Molinists, 44
Monad, 45, 54
Moss, 17, 22
Murray, Gilbert, 4

Natural theology, 25, 85, 122
Neoplatonism, 14
Nestorius, 17
Newman, 82
Newton, 52
Nicholas I, Pope, 24
Nietzsche, 31
Nominalism, 24
Non-ego, 52

Oesterley and Robinson, 4
Oman, J., 71ff, 117f, 151
Opinion, 11
Origen, 14
Ormuzd, 2
Orthodoxy, 20
Orthodoxy, Catholic, 45

Papacy, 18, 24, 26, 29, 57f, 107ff
Parent and child, 96
Parmenides, 6, 13
Paul, St, 34
Paul of Samosata, 14
Persia, 2, 103
Peters, R., 38
Philosophical theology, 86ff
Philosopher king, 10
Philosophy and theology, 61ff
Pietists, 62
'Placets of God', 33

Plato, 7, 9ff, 12, 28, 43, 93, 138, 148
Platonic myth, 138
Positivism, theological, 85
Potentiality, 12
Prophets, 4, 102f
Protagoras, 7
Protestantenverein, 125f
Pythagoreans, 111

Quakers, 111

Rameses II, 3
Rational criteria, 69f
Rationalism, 23, 38ff, 48, 53, 64
Raven, C. E., 14, 65
Reid, J. K. S., 107, 110
Reid, T., 39
Religion of Jesus, 79, 121
Republic of Plato, 9ff, 19, 138
Revelation, 33, 55, 85ff, 122f
Rich, Canon E. C., 82
Robertson, T. H., 31
Robin, 9
Rogers, 25
Rousseau, 52
Russell, 50, 91

Scharp, 58
Scheiner, 50
Schleiermacher, 62
Schoolmaster, 131f
Socrates, 6, 7ff, 111
Sophists, 6f
Sorley, 38

Sovereignty, 36f, 147
Subjectivism, 54, 56, 59, 60, 61ff, 89
Submissiveness, 96, 98

Tabula rasa, 43
Temple, William, 86
Thales, 1
Theodicy, 54
Theological circle, 123
Thrasymachus, 19
Thucydides, 5
Tillich, 73, 87
Toynbee, 20
Tradition, 8, 19, 28, 34, 105ff
Transubstantiation, 106
Trent, Council of, 58
Truth, twofold, 31, 53f

Vandals, 20
Voltaire, 46
Vorandenheit, 88

Weber, 99f
Wesley, John, 62ff, 112
Will, 52, 55, 74, 76, 118, 120, 129ff, 137f
Wolf, de, 23, 25
Word of God, The, 58ff, 84ff, 122ff, 151
Wolfenden, 81

Yorkist, anonymous, 26

Zeno, 7
Zoroastrianism, 2
Zwingli, 59

www.ingramcontent.com/pod-product-compliance
Lightning Source LLC
Chambersburg PA
CBHW071504150426
43191CB00009B/1408